CCNP

Routing and Switching

300-135 Troubleshooting
and Maintaining
Cisco IP Networks (TSHOOT)

CCNP-TSHOOT

2017

TSHOOT GUIDE/WHAT TO EXPECT ON THE EXAMINATION

The TSHOOT 300-135 (TSHOOT v2.0) exam has been used to replace the old TSHOOT 642-832 exam so this article is devoted for candidates who took this exam sharing their experience.

Exam's Structure:

+ 6 Multiple choice questions

+ 1 Simlet

+ 12 lab Questions with the same network topology (13 troubleshooting tickets or you can call it one "big" question). Each lab-sim is called a ticket and you can solve them in any order you like.

Topics of the lab-sims:

1- IPv6

2- OSPF

3- OSPFv3

4- Frame Relay

5- GRE

6- EtherChannel

7- RIPng

8- EIGRP

9- Redistribution

10- NTP

11- NAT

12- BGP

13- HSRP

14- STP

15- DHCP

The problems are rather simple. For example wrong IP assignment, disable or enable a command, authentication…

In each tickets you will have to answers three types of questions:

+ Which device causes problem

+ Which technology is used

+ How to fix it

When you press Done to finish each case, you can't go back.

A demo of the TSHOOT Exam can be found at:
http://www.cisco.com/web/learning/le3/le2/le37/le10/tshoot_demo.html

Note:

+ In the new TSHOOTv2, you cannnot use the "Abort" button anymore. Therefore you cannot check the configuration of another ticket before completing the current ticket.

Below are the topologies of the real TSHOOT exam, you are allowed to study these topologies before taking the exam. It surely saves you some invaluable time when sitting in the exam room.

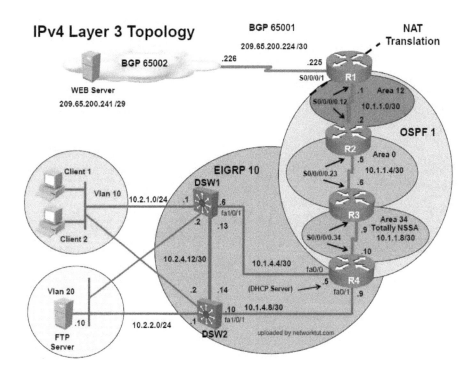

IPv6 Layer 3 Topology

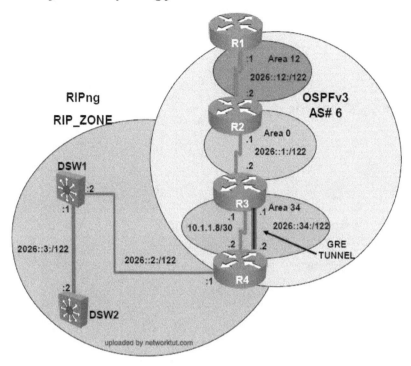

Layer 2-3 Topology

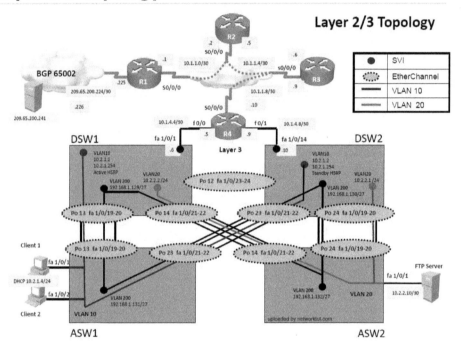

FAQ

TSHOOT is one of the three exams in the CCNP certification. The TSHOOT exam is a chance for you to review your knowledge about ROUTE & SWITCH exams and test your troubleshooting skill. From the comments here and other places, this article tries to summarize all the TSHOOT frequently asked questions to save you some time. Please feel free to ask anything that you are unclear about TSHOOT so that all of us can help you. I will update this article frequently to bring you the newest information about this exam.

1. How much does the TSHOOT Exam 300-135 cost? And the passing score of TSHOOT?

It now costs $300.

The passing score of TSHOOTv2 is 846/1000

2. Please tell me how many questions in the real TSHOOT exam, and how much time to answer them?

Unlike other Cisco exams, the TSHOOT exam tests your ability to troubleshoot the problem so in this exam you have to solve 3 multiple choice questions (or 2 multiple choice questions and 1 drag and drop question) and troubleshooting 13 "tickets". Each ticket is a problem about a specific technology used in Cisco routers or switches.

You will have 135 minutes to answer them. If your native language is not English, Cisco allows you a 30-minute exam time extension (165 minutes in total).

3. Am I allowed to study the topology used in the real exam and where can I find it ?

Yes, you are! Because the purpose of this exam is testing a candidate's ability to troubleshoot issues, not to understand a complex topology so Cisco publicizes the topology used in the real TSHOOT exam.

To save time on the exam, and to better understand the topology used in all of the trouble tickets, you should spend time familiarizing yourself with the topology used in the exam.

4. Where can I find the demo of this exam?

There is a very good demo of TSHOOT exam published by Cisco and you can find it at http://www.cisco.com/web/learning/le3/le2/le37/le10/tshoot_demo.html. But notice that the topology in this link is not the topology used in the real exam. This demo is also a good practical topology and we also explained about the configuration of this demo in four articles: Frame Relay Point-to-Point SubInterface GNS3 Lab, EIGRP over Frame Relay and EIGRP Redistribute Lab, VLAN Routing and HSRP IP Route Tracking.

5. During the exam, we must only identify the problem or we must also make the correct configuration?

We are only allowed to choose the solution for the problem. **We are not allowed to make any changes on the routers and switches**. You cannot enter global configuration mode (config)# either. You have to answer three types of questions:

+ Which device causes problem

+ Which technology is used

+ How to fix it

6. Can someone please tell me in the real exam it gives the ticket names just like in this site (for example "Ticket 1 – OSPF Authentication ") or is it going to say ticket 1 , ticket 2 only?

It only says ticket 1, ticket 2 only. In most cases you have to use the "show running-config" command to find out the wrong configuration.

7. Can I go back in the TSHOOT exam?

As shown in the above question, you can press "Previous Question" to go back to previous questions in the same ticket only. If you press "Done" button then you can't come back to this ticket anymore.

Note: In TSHOOT 300-135 (TSHOOTv2), the "Abort" button no longer exists. That means you cannot cancel a ticket after choosing it. You have to complete that ticket before moving to another one.

8. Can we take TSHOOT exam before the ROUTE or SWITCH exam?

Yes, you can. There is no order to take these exams. But the TSHOOT exam tests your skills to troubleshoot router & switch errors so I highly recommend you take the ROUTE and SWITCH exams first. The TSHOOT exam is very good to review your knowledge of what you learned in ROUTE & SWITCH.

9. Can I solve the tickets in any order I want, for example, I solve Ticket 8 first, then Ticket 3, Ticket 1...?

Yes, you can solve them in any order until you click Done button. After clicking Done you cannot go back to this ticket again. Also notice that when you entering a Ticket, you have to solve it (answer all 3 questions) before moving to another ticket.

10. As I see there are 3 topologies in the exam. My question is to how to find which topology to use when doing a troubleshooting

ticket. Does it clearly state in exam which topology to use (layer 2 or layer 3, for example)?

In the exam, it doesn't say clearly which topology you need to use.

"There is no really best way to choose which topology to use.

This is my style:

Most of the time I was using the IPv4 topology as it contains most of the nodes with ip addresses and in the cause of your troubleshooting and you discovered that you need more details on the ASW1 & 2 switches that is when I used the Layer 2 topology except for the IPv6 topology.

Any node on IPv4 topology that is in Layer 2 topology have same configuration irrespective of where you click on the nodes.

Study all tickets here and use the following elimination style below:

List out all the trouble ticket on the white little board you will be giving and tick each ticket as you answer them because this will let you know which tickets are remaining to look out for."

11. In the exam can I use "traceroute" or "tracert" command?

According to some reports, "tracert" commands cannot be used on Clients but "traceroute" command can be used on DSW1. But of course you can use "ping" command. According to some candidates' reports on the exam, maybe you should not believe too much on the output of the traceroute command in the exam.

12. Please let me know in the exam can we issue "pipe" commands such as: sh run | section eigrp; sh run | begin router?

No, you cannot use "pipe" commands in the TSHOOT exam.

13. Does each ticket state it is an IPv4 or IPv6 issue?

Yes, it does! But it does not clearly state that. Please read each ticket carefully, if it states like this "loopback address on R1 (2026::111:1) is not able to ping the loopback address on DSW2 (2026::102:1)" then surely it is an IPv6 ticket. Otherwise it is an IPv4 ticket.

14. Why in each ticket I only see the same description, same wording, either ticket 1, 2 or 3. How can I see the difference or the problem of each ticket?

The descriptions of each ticket are very identical to each other. In general the very long description can be summarized "Client 1 cannot ping the 209.65.200.241" (for IPv4 ticket), that's all! So you have to use your troubleshooting skill to find out where the issue (it is also the meaning of this exam – TSHOOT). The only obvious difference among the tickets is the statement "loopback address on R1 (2026::111:1) is not able to ping the loopback address on DSW2 (2026::102:1)", which indicates an IPv6 ticket.

A guide for the TSHOOT Exam

For the TSHOOTv2 exam we will encounter:

+ 1 Simlet (small troubleshooting sim)

+ 6 Multiple Choice Questions

+ 12 Troubleshooting Tickets

Below is a summary of 16 Tickets you will see in the exam:

Device	Error Description
ASW1	1. Access port not in VLAN 10
	2. Port Channel not allowing VLAN 10
DSW1	1. HSRP track 10 (removed)
	2. VLAN filter
R1	1. Wrong IP of BGP neighbor (removed)
	2. NAT Inside misconfigured
	3. WAN access-list statement missing
	4. OSPF Authentication
R2	1. IPv6: enable OSPF
R3	1. IPv6: remove "tunnel mode ipv6"
R4	1. EIGRP – wrong AS (removed)
	2. Redistribute ("to" & ->)

	3. DHCP IP Helper-address
	4. EIGRP Passive Interface
	5. missing Redistribution from RIPng to OSPFv3

Special note: In the old TSHOOT exam there were some tickets in which Client 1 & 2 got APIPA addresses (169.254.x.x) because they used DHCP to request their IP addresses. In the new TSHOOTv2 exam, Client1 & 2 IP addresses are statically assigned so you will not see APIPA addresses any more. Client1 & 2 always have IP addresses of 10.2.1.3 & 10.2.1.4.

Notice that in the exam, the tickets are randomly given so the best way to troubleshooting is to try pinging to all the devices from nearest to farthest from the client until you don't receive the replies.

In each ticket you will have to answers three types of questions:

+ Which device causes problem

+ Which technology is used

+ How to fix it

One more thing to remember: you can only use "show" commands to find out the problems and you are not allowed to make any changes in the configuration. In fact, in the exam you can not enter the global configuration mode!

VLAN Routing

In this article we will discuss about the configuration on the switches of the TSHOOT Demo ticket. We post the topology here for your reference.

Layer2/3 topology

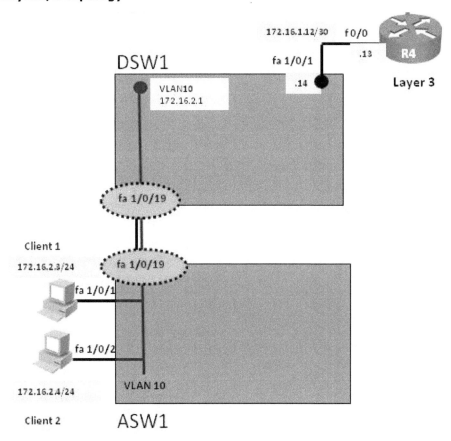

Main Configuration on DSW1 and ASW1

DSW1:
ip routing
vtp mode transparent
!
vlan 10
name CLIENT_VLAN
!
vlan 98
name NATIVE_VLAN
!
vlan 99
name PARKING_LOT
!
interface range Fa1/0/2 – 18,
Fa1/0/20 – 48, Gi1/0/1 – 4
switchport access vlan 99
switchport mode access
shutdown
!
interface FastEthernet1/0/1
description Link to R4
no switchport
ip address 172.16.1.14
255.255.255.252
!
interface FastEthernet1/0/19
description Trunk to ASW1
switchport access vlan 99
switchport trunk encapsulation
dot1q
switchport trunk native vlan 98
switchport trunk allowed vlan
10,98
switchport mode trunk
!
interface Vlan10
ip address 172.16.2.1
255.255.255.0
!
router eigrp 16
network 172.16.1.0 0.0.0.255
network 172.16.2.0 0.0.0.255
passive-interface default
no passive-interface
FastEthernet0/1

ASW1:
vtp mode transparent
!
vlan 10
name CLIENT_VLAN
!
vlan 98
name NATIVE_VLAN
!
vlan 99
name PARKING_LOT
!
interface FastEthernet1/0/1
switchport access vlan 10
switchport mode access
spanning-tree portfast
!
interface FastEthernet1/0/2
switchport access vlan 10
switchport mode access
spanning-tree portfast
!
interface range Fa1/0/3 – 18,
Fa1/0/20 – 48, Gi1/0/1 – 4
switchport access vlan 99
switchport mode access
shutdown
!
interface FastEthernet1/0/19
description Link to DSW1
switchport trunk encapsulation
dot1q
switchport trunk native vlan 98
switchport trunk allowed vlan
10,98
switchport mode trunk

From the output above we learn that:

+ VTP is disabled on both switches.

+ DSW1: running EIGRP (Layer 3 switch) while ASW1 is pure layer 2 switch

+ Configuration VLANs on both switches as follows:

a) VLAN 10: CLIENT_VLAN (two computers are assigned to this VLAN)

b) VLAN 98: NATIVE_VLAN (no ports are assigned to this VLAN. This VLAN exists just to make sure traffic from other VLANs are tagged)

c) VLAN 99: PARKING_LOT (unused ports are assigned to this VLAN)

+ Fa1/0/19 is the trunking port between two switches

+ Only VLAN 10 and 98 are allowed to go through 2 switches.

+ Default gateway on two PCs are 172.16.2.1 which is the IP address of Interface VLAN 10 on DSW1.

+ EIGRP updated is only sent and received on fa1/0/1 which connects from DSW1 to R4

+ On ASW1, spanning-tree PortFast feature is enabled on fa1/0/1 & fa1/0/2 which are connected to two PCs.

Note: On DSW1, under interface Fa1/0/19 we can see this command:

switchport access vlan 99

but this port is set as trunk port (switchport mode trunk) so how can a command for access port be there? Well, in fact we have set this port to trunk mode so the **switchport access vlan 99** command has no effect at all. It only affects when you change this port to an access port and this port would be assigned to VLAN 99.

The IP address of interface VLAN 10 (172.16.2.1/24) is set as the default gateway on Host 1 & Host 2. In general, a Switch Virtual Interface (SVI) represents a logical Layer 3 interface on a switch and it can be used to interconnect Layer 3 networks using routing protocols (like RIP, OSPF, EIGRP...). When packets reach this SVI, the Layer 3 switch will look up in its routing table to see if there is an entry to route the packets to the destination. In this case, packets sent from Host 1 & 2 reach 172.16.2.1 (because this IP is also the default gateway set on Host 1 & 2), then DSW1 looks up in its routing table for a suitable entry to the destination.

Quick reminder: VLAN interfaces or switched virtual interfaces (SVI) are logical layer 3 routable interface. Generally, SVIs are often used to accomplish InterVLAN routing on a Layer 3 switch. From there, you would point the client devices to the VLAN interface to use as it's default gateway. When a packet arrives on that interface, the Layer 3 switch will do a routing table lookup and perform routing process like a normal packet.

In the next part we will try to do above topology in Packet Tracer. But Packet Tracer does not understand redistribute static route into EIGRP so we simplify the configuration by running EIGRP on all routers.

Physical topology

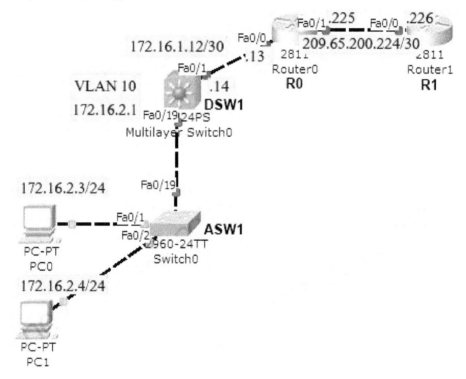

Tasks in the lab:

+ VTP is disabled on both switches.

+ DSW1: running EIGRP (Layer 3 switch) while ASW1 is pure layer 2 switch

+ Configuration VLANs on both switches as follows:

a) VLAN 10: CLIENT_VLAN (two computers are assigned to this VLAN)

b) VLAN 98: NATIVE_VLAN (no ports are assigned to this VLAN. This VLAN exists just to make sure traffic from other VLANs are tagged)

c) VLAN 99: PARKING_LOT (unused ports are assigned to this VLAN)

+ Fa0/19 is the trunking port between two switches

+ Only VLAN 10 and 98 are allowed to go through 2 switches.

+ Default gateway on two PCs are 172.16.2.1 which is the IP address of Interface VLAN 10 on DSW1.

+ EIGRP updated is only sent and received on fa0/1 which connects from DSW1 to R4

+ On ASW1, spanning-tree PortFast feature is enabled on fa0/1 & fa0/2 which are connected to two PCs.

Configuration

ASW1
```
hostname ASW1
!
vtp mode transparent
!
vlan 10
name CLIENT_VLAN
!
vlan 98
name NATIVE_VLAN
!
vlan 99
name PARKING_LOT
!
interface FastEthernet0/1
switchport access vlan 10
switchport mode access
spanning-tree portfast
!
interface FastEthernet0/2
switchport access vlan 10
switchport mode access
spanning-tree portfast
!
interface FastEthernet0/19
description Link to DSW1
switchport trunk encapsulation
dot1q
switchport trunk native vlan 98
switchport trunk allowed vlan
10,98
switchport mode trunk
```

DSW1
```
hostname DSW1
ip routing
!
vtp mode transparent
!
vlan 10
name CLIENT_VLAN
!
vlan 98
name NATIVE_VLAN
!
vlan 99
name PARKING_LOT
!
interface FastEthernet0/1
description Link to R4
no switchport
ip address 172.16.1.14
255.255.255.252
no shutdown
!
interface FastEthernet0/19
description Trunk to ASW1
switchport access vlan 99
switchport trunk encapsulation
dot1q
switchport trunk native vlan 98
switchport trunk allowed vlan
10,98
switchport mode trunk
!
interface Vlan10
ip address 172.16.2.1
255.255.255.0
!
router eigrp 16
network 172.16.1.0 0.0.0.255
network 172.16.2.0 0.0.0.255
passive-interface default
no passive-interface
FastEthernet0/1
```

RO	R1
hostname R0	hostname R1
!	!
interface FastEthernet0/0	interface FastEthernet0/0
ip address 172.16.1.13	ip address 209.65.200.226
255.255.255.252	255.255.255.252
no shutdown	no shutdown
!	!
interface FastEthernet0/1	router eigrp 16
ip address 209.65.200.225	network 209.65.200.0
255.255.255.252	
no shutdown	
!	
router eigrp 16	
network 172.16.0.0	
network 209.65.200.0	

Also configure IP addresses and default gateways of the two computers as follows:

PC0	PC1
IP: 172.16.2.3/24	IP: 172.16.2.4/24
Default gateway: 172.16.2.1	Default gateway: 172.16.2.1

Now two hosts can ping 209.65.200.226.

The Packet Tracer initial and final configs can be downloaded here:

Initial Configs:

https://www.dropbox.com/s/jadvekr2r3ucnj7/TSHOOT_demo_VLAN_switches_initial.zip?dl=0

Final Configs:

https://www.dropbox.com/s/opgwm3u4wlu2n37/TSHOOT_demo_VLAN_switches_finalConfigs.zip?dl=0

HSRP IP Route Tracking

In this article we will discuss about HSRP and do a lab on it.

Quick reminder about HSRP

+ Hot Standby Router Protocol (HSRP) is a Cisco proprietary protocol.

+ With HSRP, two or more devices support a virtual router with a fictitious MAC address and unique IP address

+ Hosts use this IP address as their default gateway and the MAC address for the Layer 2 header

+ The virtual router's MAC address is 0000.0c07.ACxx , in which xx is the HSRP group. Multiple groups (virtual routers) are allowed.

+ The Active router forwards traffic. The Standby router is backup and monitors periodic hellos (multicast to 224.0.0.2,

UDP port 1985) to detect a failure of the active router.

+ The active router is chosen because it has the highest HSRP priority (default priority is 100). In case of a tie, the router

with the highest configured IP address wins the election

+ A new router with a higher priority does not cause an election unless it is configured to preempt.

HSRP States

+ Initial: HSRP is not running.

+ Learn: The router does not know the virtual IP address and is waiting to hear from the active router.

+ Listen: The router knows the IP and MAC of the virtual router, but it is not the active or standby router.

+ Speak: Router sends periodic HSRP hellos and participates in the election of the active router.

+ Standby: Router monitors hellos from active router and assumes responsibility if active router fails.

+ Active:Router forwards packets on behalf of the virtual router.

Load balancing traffic across two uplinks to two HSRP routers with a single HSRP group is not possible. The trick is to use two

HSRP groups:

+ One group assigns an active router to one switch.

+ The other group assigns another active router to the other switch.

(Reference: SWITCH official Certification Guide)

That is all for the boring HSRP theory, let do a lab to understand more about HSRP! We will use the topology below for this lab:

Loopback0:4.4.4.4

All subnet masks are /24

R4

f0/0   f1/0

24.24.24.0   34.34.34.0

f1/0   f1/0

R2   R3

f0/0   f0/0

123.123.123.2   123.123.123.3

SW1

1

f0/0   123.123.123.1

R1

IOS used: c3640-jk9s-mz.124-16.bin

Tasks in this lab:

+ Configure IP addresses as shown and run EIGRP on R2, R3, R4

+ Configure HSRP: R2 is the Active HSRP while R3 is the Standby HSRP

+ Tracking route to 4.4.4.4, traffic should goes to R3 once the route to 4.4.4.4 is lost in R2 or the metric to R4's loopback interface increases.

IP Address and EIGRP Configuration

R1 (configured as a host) no ip routing ip default-gateway 123.123.123.254 //This is the virtual IP of HSRP group interface FastEthernet0/0 ip address 123.123.123.1 255.255.255.0 no shutdown	**R2** interface FastEthernet0/0 ip address 123.123.123.2 255.255.255.0 no shutdown ! interface FastEthernet1/0 ip address 24.24.24.2 255.255.255.0 no shutdown ! router eigrp 1 network 24.0.0.0 network 123.0.0.0
R3 interface FastEthernet0/0 ip address 123.123.123.3 255.255.255.0 no shutdown ! interface FastEthernet1/0 ip address 34.34.34.3 255.255.255.0 no shutdown ! router eigrp 1 network 34.0.0.0 network 123.0.0.0	**R4** interface Loopback0 ip address 4.4.4.4 255.255.255.0 ! interface FastEthernet0/0 ip address 24.24.24.4 255.255.255.0 no shutdown ! interface FastEthernet1/0 ip address 34.34.34.4 255.255.255.0 no shutdown ! router eigrp 1 network 4.0.0.0 network 24.0.0.0 network 34.0.0.0

HSRP Configuration

R2	**R3**
interface FastEthernet0/0	interface FastEthernet0/0
standby 10 ip 123.123.123.254	standby 10 ip 123.123.123.254
standby 10 priority 200	standby 10 priority 150
standby 10 preempt	standby 10 preempt

Note: The virtual IP address of HSRP group must be in the same subnet of the
IP address on this interface (Fa0/0)

After entering above commands we will see R2 takes **Active** state after going from **Speak** to **Standby**:

%HSRP-5-STATECHANGE: FastEthernet0/0 Grp 10 state Speak -> Standby

*Mar 1 00:10:22.487: %HSRP-5-STATECHANGE: FastEthernet0/0 Grp 10 state Standby -> Active

*Mar 1 00:10:22.871: %SYS-5-CONFIG_I: Configured from console by console

The "show standby" command on R2 confirms its state:

```
R2#show standby
FastEthernet0/0 - Group 10
  State is Active
    2 state changes, last state change 00:01:59
  Virtual IP address is 123.123.123.254
  Active virtual MAC address is 0000.0c07.ac0a
    Local virtual MAC address is 0000.0c07.ac0a (v1 default)
  Hello time 3 sec, hold time 10 sec
    Next hello sent in 0.424 secs
  Preemption enabled
  Active router is local
  Standby router is 123.123.123.3, priority 150 (expires in 9.440 sec)
  Priority 200 (configured 200)
  IP redundancy name is "hsrp-Fa0/0-10" (default)
```

Now R2 is in HSRP Active state with virtual MAC address of 00000c07.ac0a. Notice that the last two numbers of the MAC address (0a) is the HSRP group number in hexadecimal form (0a in hexa = 10 in decimal)

The "show standby" command on R3 reveals it is in **Standby** state:

```
R3#show standby
FastEthernet0/0 - Group 10
  State is Standby
    1 state change, last state change 00:03:30
  Virtual IP address is 123.123.123.254
  Active virtual MAC address is 0000.0c07.ac0a
    Local virtual MAC address is 0000.0c07.ac0a (v1 default)
  Hello time 3 sec, hold time 10 sec
    Next hello sent in 2.196 secs
  Preemption enabled
  Active router is 123.123.123.2, priority 200 (expires in 7.204 sec)
  Standby router is local
  Priority 150 (configured 150)
  IP redundancy name is "hsrp-Fa0/0-10" (default)
```

Now we will see what happens if we turn off interface Fa0/0 on R2:

R2(config)#interface fa0/0

R2(config-if)#shutdown

```
R2#show standby
FastEthernet0/0 - Group 10
  State is Init (interface down)
    3 state changes, last state change 00:00:26
  Virtual IP address is 123.123.123.254
  Active virtual MAC address is unknown
    Local virtual MAC address is 0000.0c07.ac0a (v1 default)
  Hello time 3 sec, hold time 10 sec
  Preemption enabled
  Active router is unknown
  Standby router is unknown
  Priority 200 (configured 200)
  IP redundancy name is "hsrp-Fa0/0-10" (default)
```

```
R3#show standby
FastEthernet0/0 - Group 10
  State is Active
    2 state changes, last state change 00:02:39
  Virtual IP address is 123.123.123.254
  Active virtual MAC address is 0000.0c07.ac0a
    Local virtual MAC address is 0000.0c07.ac0a (v1 default)
  Hello time 3 sec, hold time 10 sec
    Next hello sent in 2.356 secs
  Preemption enabled
  Active router is local
  Standby router is unknown
  Priority 150 (configured 150)
  IP redundancy name is "hsrp-Fa0/0-10" (default)
```

As we can see, the HSRP state of R2 went back to **Init** while the HSRP state of R3 moved to **Active**.

HSRP Tracking IP Route

In this part instead of tracking an interface going up or down we can track if the metric of a route to a destination changes or not. In particular we will try to track the route to the loopback interface of R4 (4.4.4.4). First we should check the routing table of R2:

```
R2#show ip route
Codes: C - connected, S - static, R - RIP, M - mobile, B - BGP
       D - EIGRP, EX - EIGRP external, O - OSPF, IA - OSPF inter area
       N1 - OSPF NSSA external type 1, N2 - OSPF NSSA external type 2
       E1 - OSPF external type 1, E2 - OSPF external type 2
       i - IS-IS, su - IS-IS summary, L1 - IS-IS level-1, L2 - IS-IS level-2
       ia - IS-IS inter area, * - candidate default, U - per-user static route
       o - ODR, P - periodic downloaded static route

Gateway of last resort is not set

D     34.0.0.0/8 [90/30720] via 123.123.123.3, 00:19:19, FastEthernet0/0
                  [90/30720] via 24.24.24.4, 00:19:19, FastEthernet1/0
D     4.0.0.0/8 [90/156160] via 24.24.24.4, 00:19:19, FastEthernet1/0
      24.0.0.0/8 is variably subnetted, 2 subnets, 2 masks
C        24.24.24.0/24 is directly connected, FastEthernet1/0
D        24.0.0.0/8 is a summary, 00:19:22, Null0
      123.0.0.0/8 is variably subnetted, 2 subnets, 2 masks
C        123.123.123.0/24 is directly connected, FastEthernet0/0
D        123.0.0.0/8 is a summary, 00:19:24, Null0
```

We learn that the metric to the loopback interface of R4 (4.4.4.4) is 156160 and is summarized to 4.0.0.0/8 prefix because EIGRP summarizes route by default.

Now add tracking ip routing to R2

R2(config)#track 1 ip route 4.0.0.0 255.0.0.0 metric threshold

R2(config-track)#threshold metric up 61 down 62

and on interface fa0/0 add these commands to apply the track:

R2(config)#interface fa0/0

R2(config-if)#standby 10 track 1 decrement 60

The command **track ip route metric threshold** is used to track the metric change of a route. For example in this case the second command **threshold metric up 61 down 62** specifies the low and high thresholds.

up: Specifies the up threshold. The state is up if the scaled metric for that route is less than or equal to the up threshold. The default up threshold is 254.

down: Specifies the down threshold. The state is down if the scaled metric for that route is greater than or equal to the down threshold. The default down threshold is 255.

Then, how do we indicate the **up** value should be 61 and **down** value should be 62? This is because EIGRP routes are scaled by means of 2560 so if we divide the EIGRP metric (156160 in this case) by 2560 we will get 61 (156160 / 2560 = 61). 2560 is the default metric resolution value for EIGRP and can be modified by the **track resolution** command (for example: track resolution ip route eigrp 400). The table below lists the metric resolution for popular routing protocols.

Routing protocol	Metric Resolution
Static	10
EIGRP	2560
OSPF	1
RIP	is scaled directly to the range from 0 to 255 because its maximum metric is less than 255

In this case if the metric for route to 4.0.0.0/8 in the routing table is less than or equal to 61 then the state is up. If the metric is greater or equal to 62, the state is down. We can verify if the track is working correctly by the **show track** command.

```
R2#show track
Track 1
   IP route 4.0.0.0 255.0.0.0 metric threshold
   Metric threshold is Up (EIGRP/156160/61)
      2 changes, last change 00:00:36
   Metric threshold down 62 up 61
   First-hop interface is FastEthernet1/0
   Tracked by:
      HSRP FastEthernet0/0 10
```

When the state is Down, R2's priority will be deduced by 60: 200 – 60 = 140 which is less than the priority of R3 (150) -> R3 will take the Active state of R2.

```
R2#show standby
FastEthernet0/0 - Group 10
  State is Standby
    7 state changes, last state change 00:03:25
  Virtual IP address is 123.123.123.254
  Active virtual MAC address is 0000.0c07.ac0a
    Local virtual MAC address is 0000.0c07.ac0a (v1 default)
  Hello time 3 sec, hold time 10 sec
    Next hello sent in 1.964 secs
  Preemption enabled
  Active router is 123.123.123.3, priority 150 (expires in 7.996 sec)
  Standby router is local
  Priority 140 (configured 200)
    Track object 1 state Down decrement 60
  IP redundancy name is "hsrp-Fa0/0-10" (default)

R3#show standby
FastEthernet0/0 - Group 10
  State is Active
    5 state changes, last state change 00:05:56
  Virtual IP address is 123.123.123.254
  Active virtual MAC address is 0000.0c07.ac0a
    Local virtual MAC address is 0000.0c07.ac0a (v1 default)
  Hello time 3 sec, hold time 10 sec
    Next hello sent in 0.560 secs
  Preemption enabled
  Active router is local
  Standby router is 123.123.123.2, priority 140 (expires in 8.592 sec)
  Priority 150 (configured 150)
  IP redundancy name is "hsrp-Fa0/0-10" (default)
```

A very important note we wish to mention here is: the route for tracking should be exactly same as displayed in the routing table or the track would go down because no route is found. For example if we try tracking the route to the more specific route 4.4.4.0/24 or 4.4.4.4/24 the track would go down because EIGRP summarizes route by default before advertising through another major network. Let's try this!

R2(config)#no track 1 ip route 4.0.0.0 255.0.0.0 metric threshold

R2(config)#track 1 ip route 4.4.4.0 255.255.255.0 metric threshold

R2(config-track)#threshold metric up 61 down 62

Now check if the track is working or not:

```
R2#show track
Track 1
   IP route 4.4.4.0 255.255.255.0 metric threshold
   Metric threshold is Down (no route)
      1 change, last change 00:00:25
   Metric threshold down 62 up 61
   First-hop interface is unknown
   Tracked by:
      HSRP FastEthernet0/0 10
```

The track on R2 goes down so R2's priority is reduced by 60 which causes R3 takes the Active state.

In this case if we wish to bring up the track route to 4.4.4.0/24 we just need to use the "no auto-summary" command on R4 which causes R4 to advertise the more specific route of 4.4.4.0/24.

R4(config)#router eigrp 1

R4(config-router)#no auto-summary

Now R4 advertises the detailed 4.4.4.0/24 network and it matches with our tracking process so the tracking process will go up.

```
R2#show ip route
Codes: C - connected, S - static, R - RIP, M - mobile, B - BGP
       D - EIGRP, EX - EIGRP external, O - OSPF, IA - OSPF inter area
       N1 - OSPF NSSA external type 1, N2 - OSPF NSSA external type 2
       E1 - OSPF external type 1, E2 - OSPF external type 2
       i - IS-IS, su - IS-IS summary, L1 - IS-IS level-1, L2 - IS-IS level-2
       ia - IS-IS inter area, * - candidate default, U - per-user static route
       o - ODR, P - periodic downloaded static route

Gateway of last resort is not set

     34.0.0.0/8 is variably subnetted, 2 subnets, 2 masks
D       34.34.34.0/24 [90/30720] via 24.24.24.4, 00:01:26, FastEthernet1/0
D       34.0.0.0/8 [90/30720] via 123.123.123.3, 00:01:26, FastEthernet0/0
     4.0.0.0/24 is subnetted, 1 subnets
D       4.4.4.0 [90/156160] via 24.24.24.4, 00:01:26, FastEthernet1/0
     24.0.0.0/8 is variably subnetted, 2 subnets, 2 masks
C       24.24.24.0/24 is directly connected, FastEthernet1/0
D       24.0.0.0/8 is a summary, 00:01:26, Null0
     123.0.0.0/8 is variably subnetted, 2 subnets, 2 masks
C       123.123.123.0/24 is directly connected, FastEthernet0/0
D       123.0.0.0/8 is a summary, 00:39:39, Null0
```

```
R2#show track
Track 1
  IP route 4.4.4.0 255.255.255.0 metric threshold
  Metric threshold is Up (EIGRP/156160/61)
    2 changes, last change 00:02:36
  Metric threshold down 62 up 61
  First-hop interface is FastEthernet1/0
  Tracked by:
    HSRP FastEthernet0/0 10
```

The GNS3 initial and final configs can be downloaded here:

Initial Configs:

https://www.dropbox.com/s/lh23bahfgvp2rzn/HSRP_initial.zip?dl=0

Final Configs:

https://www.dropbox.com/s/g4ag9dia76zatbj/HSRP_finalConfigs.zip?dl=0

(Good reference:
http://www.cisco.com/en/US/docs/ios/12_2sb/feature/guide/sbaiptrk.html)

Frame Relay Point-to-Point SubInterface GNS3 Lab

In this lab we will try to run a Frame Relay topology same as the one posted in TSHOOT demo ticket. The logical and physical topologies of this lab are shown below:

Logical topology:

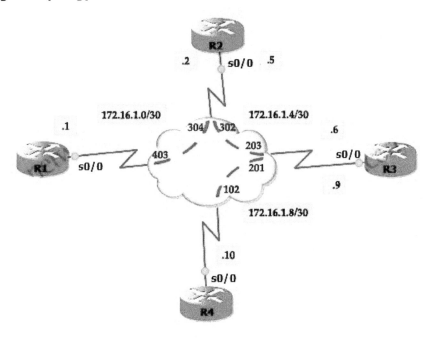

Tasks in this lab:

+ Configure static mappings on R1 and R4.

+ Configure point-to-point subinterface on R2 & R3.

+ All routers must be able to ping themselves.

Physical topology:

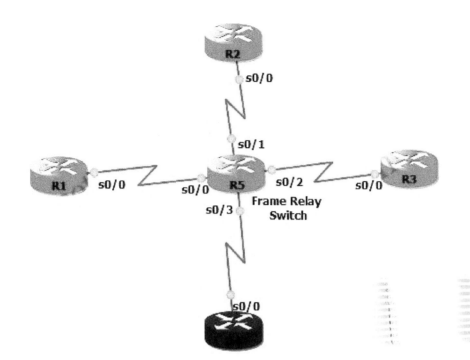

IOS used in this lab: **c3640-jk9s-mz.124-16.bin**

We will use a router (R5) to simulate the Frame Relay switch instead of using a Frame Relay Switch in GNS3. First we will configure the Frame Relay switch with the DLCIs shown above. In fact the DLCIs in the topology are not very logical, especially DLCIs 304 & 403 for the links between R1 & R2, but well... let's configure them.

Note: If you are not sure about Frame Relay theory, please read my Frame Relay tutorial first.

Configuration

Configure Frame Relay Switch:

We should change the name of R5 to FRSW (Frame Relay Switch).

R5(config)#**hostname FRSW**

The very first command to turn on the frame relay switching feature on FRSW:

FRSW(config)#**frame-relay switching**

FRSW(config)#int s0/0 FRSW(config-if)#encapsulation frame-relay FRSW(config-if)#frame-relay intf-type dce FRSW(config-if)#clock rate 64000 FRSW(config-if)#frame-relay route 403 interface serial 0/1 304 FRSW(config-if)#no shutdown	FRSW(config)#int s0/1 FRSW(config-if)#encapsulation frame-relay FRSW(config-if)#frame-relay intf-type dce FRSW(config-if)#clock rate 64000 FRSW(config-if)#frame-relay route 304 interface serial 0/0 403 FRSW(config-if)#frame-relay route 302 interface serial 0/2 203 FRSW(config-if)#no shutdown
FRSW(config)#int s0/2 FRSW(config-if)#encapsulation frame-relay FRSW(config-if)#frame-relay intf-type dce FRSW(config-if)#clock rate 64000 FRSW(config-if)#frame-relay route 203 interface serial 0/1 302 FRSW(config-if)#frame-relay route 201 interface serial 0/3 102 FRSW(config-if)#no shutdown	FRSW(config)#int s0/3 FRSW(config-if)#encapsulation frame-relay FRSW(config-if)#frame-relay intf-type dce FRSW(config-if)#clock rate 64000 FRSW(config-if)#frame-relay route 102 interface serial 0/2 201 FRSW(config-if)#no shutdown

+ The **frame-relay intf-type dce** command specifies the interface to handle LMI like a Frame Relay DCE device. This command also enables FRSW to function as a switch connected to a router. And the clock rate is necessary on the DCE end of the connection so we have to put it here (but in fact not all IOS versions require this, you can check or verify the DCE and clock rate with the **show controller serial x/y** command).

+ The **frame-relay route 403 interface serial 0/1 304** command means frame-relay traffic comes to FRSW which has a DLCI of 403 will be sent to interface Serial0/1 with a DLCI of 304.

Also please notice that there is no IP address configured on the Frame Relay Switch.

We can verify the configuration of the FRSW with **show frame-relay route** command:

```
FRSW#sh frame route
Input Intf      Input Dlci      Output Intf     Output Dlci     Status
Serial0/0       403             Serial0/1       304             active
Serial0/1       302             Serial0/2       203             active
Serial0/1       304             Serial0/0       403             active
Serial0/2       201             Serial0/3       102             active
Serial0/2       203             Serial0/1       302             active
Serial0/3       102             Serial0/2       201             active
```

Note: The output above is taken after all routers have been configured so if you do this command in your lab at this moment the **Status** would be **Inactive** because you have not turned on the Serial interfaces on R1, R2, R3, R4.

Configure R1, R2, R3 and R4:

First I show all the configuration but you should type them manually to see how it works instead of pasting all of them at the same time.

R1:	R2:
interface s0/0	interface Serial0/0
ip address 172.16.1.1	no ip address
255.255.255.252	encapsulation frame-relay
encapsulation frame-relay	no shutdown
no frame-relay inverse-arp	!
frame-relay map ip 172.16.1.1	interface Serial0/0.12
403 broadcast	point-to-point
frame-relay map ip 172.16.1.2	description Link to R1
403	ip address 172.16.1.2
no shutdown	255.255.255.252
(good to explain first broadcast:	frame-relay interface-dlci
https://learningnetwork.cisco.com	304
/thread/35698)	!
	interface Serial0/0.23
	point-to-point
	description Link to R3
	ip address 172.16.1.5
	255.255.255.252
	frame-relay interface-dlci
	302
R3:	**R4:**
interface Serial0/0	interface Serial0/0
no ip address	description Link to R3
encapsulation frame-relay	ip address 172.16.1.10
no frame-relay inverse-arp	255.255.255.252
no shutdown	encapsulation frame-relay
!	frame-relay map ip
interface Serial0/0.23 point-to-	172.16.1.9 102 broadcast
point	frame-relay map ip
description Link to R2	172.16.1.10 102
ip address 172.16.1.6	no frame-relay inverse-arp
255.255.255.252	no shutdown
frame-relay interface-dlci 203	
!	
interface Serial0/0.34 point-to-	
point	
description Link to R4	
ip address 172.16.1.9	
255.255.255.252	
frame-relay interface-dlci 201	

There are somethings I wish to explain. For example on R1 under interface s0/0 we see the command:

frame-relay map ip 172.16.1.1 403 broadcast

The **frame-relay map** command performs static addressing mapping and it disables Inverse ARP on the specified DLCI. This command is supported on the physical interface and it should be used when the far end Frame Relay device does not support Inverse ARP. If we choose to disable Inverse ARP, we must perform a static mapping of L2 to L3, as well as associate the DLCI to the interface.

The IP address 172.16.1.1 is the IP address of R1 itself so why do we need this command? The answer is: without this command, you cannot ping from R1 to itself (ping to it own IP address may be a lab requirement, a fun test...) because that IP address does not exist in the Frame Relay map table and Frame Relay does not know which DLCI it should use to send the frames to this destination. You can check this with the "debug frame-relay packet" command to see the error **Serial0/0:Encaps failed–no map entry link 7(IP)**. By adding a static map to the DLCI used for a neighbor, when we ping to itself, the router will send ICMP to that neighbor and the neighbor will reply back to R1.

Now let's discuss about the **broadcast** keyword in the above command. First, please notice that the "broadcast" keyword here is used for both multicast and broadcast traffic. By default, Frame Relay is a non-broadcast multiple access (NBMA) network and does not support broadcast or multicast traffic. So without the **broadcast** keyword, dynamic routing protocols such as EIGRP, OSPF and RIPv2 would not be able to advertise multicast route updates over the corresponding DLCI. Therefore we should always add this keyword in the "frame-relay map" command. But remember this: we only use one **broadcast** keyword for each DLCI regardless how many IP addresses are used along with. So the commands below:

frame-relay map ip 172.16.1.1 403 broadcast

frame-relay map ip 172.16.1.2 403

are same as:

frame-relay map ip 172.16.1.1 403

frame-relay map ip 172.16.1.2 403 broadcast

You should never use more then one broadcast keyword for one DLCI like this:

frame-relay map ip 172.16.1.1 403 broadcast

frame-relay map ip 172.16.1.2 403 broadcast

or you will end up with multiple copies of the packets being transported and received.

> Configuring static map statements (like **frame-relay map ip** command) automatically disables Inverse ARP so in the configuration of R1, the **no frame-relay inverse-arp** command is in fact not necessary.
>
> Note: Physical interfaces have Inverse ARP enabled by default

That is all explanation for R1. Next we will discuss about the configuration of R2 and R3 (they are very identical). Under subinterface (like Serial0/0.12 point-to-point on R2) we see the command:

frame-relay interface-dlci 304

We notice that in this command only the DLCI is specified and this command just associates the DLCI with the subinterface. This is because point-to-point network only connects with one remote destination. Therefore this command is mostly used under point-to-point subinterface (but it can be still used on physical interface although it has no effect because all unassigned DLCIs belong to that physical interface by default). On point-to-point subinterface, Inverse ARP requests are not sent out regardless if it is enabled on the physical interface or not. It is also not required to enable or disable Inverse ARP, because there is only a single remote destination on a PVC and discovery is not necessary. Also notice that the **frame-relay map** command is not allowed on a point-to-point subinterface.

Note: Using subinterface can avoid the split-horizon problem.

We can check which type of mapping was configured with the command "show frame-relay map":

+ **Dynamic** means the mapping was done using Inverse ARP.

+ **Static** means the mapping was done manually.

For example on R1 static mapping is being used:

```
R1#show frame-relay map
Serial0/0 (up): ip 172.16.1.2 dlci 403(0x193,0x6430), static,
               broadcast,
               CISCO, status defined, active
```

Let's check R2:

```
R2#show frame-relay map
Serial0/0.23 (up): point-to-point dlci, dlci 302(0x12E,0x48E0), broadcast
            status defined, active
Serial0/0.12 (up): point-to-point dlci, dlci 304(0x130,0x4C00), broadcast
            status defined, active
```

Hmm, on R2 we don't see the word "static" or "dynamic". There are some confusions about the "frame-relay interface-dlci" command if it belongs to dynamic mapping or static mapping. But there is an opinion saying that point-to-point does not use the principle of static or dynamic mapping so it is not listed here. Well, the decision is yours.

Also you can notice that no Layer 3 addresses are shown in above command.

On the "show frame-relay map" outputs above you can see the Frame Relay's statuses are all **active**. There are 4 PVC statuses:

+ **Active**: Both sides of the PVC are up and communicating.

+ **Inactive:** Local router received status about the DLCI from the frame-switch, the other side is down.

+ **Deleted**: Indicates a local config problem. The frame-switch has no such mapping and responded with a "deleted message".

+ **Static**: Indicates that LMI was turned off with the "no keepalives".

The outputs of the show frame-relay map command on R3 & R4 are very identical to R1 & R2, I also post here just for your reference:

```
R3#show frame-relay map
Serial0/0.23 (up): point-to-point dlci, dlci 203(0xCB,0x30B0), broadcast
          status defined, active
Serial0/0.34 (up): point-to-point dlci, dlci 201(0xC9,0x3090), broadcast
          status defined, active
```

```
R4#show frame-relay map
Serial0/0 (up): ip 172.16.1.9 dlci 102(0x66,0x1860), static,
          broadcast,
          CISCO, status defined, active
```

That's all I wish to explain, let's check if the pings work...

```
R1#ping 172.16.1.2

Type escape sequence to abort.
Sending 5, 100-byte ICMP Echos to 172.16.1.2, timeout is 2 seconds:
!!!!!
Success rate is 100 percent (5/5), round-trip min/avg/max = 12/28/52 ms
```

```
R2#ping 172.16.1.1

Type escape sequence to abort.
Sending 5, 100-byte ICMP Echos to 172.16.1.1, timeout is 2 seconds:
!!!!!
Success rate is 100 percent (5/5), round-trip min/avg/max = 16/36/68 ms
R2#ping 172.16.1.6

Type escape sequence to abort.
Sending 5, 100-byte ICMP Echos to 172.16.1.6, timeout is 2 seconds:
!!!!!
Success rate is 100 percent (5/5), round-trip min/avg/max = 16/25/44 ms
```

```
R3#ping 172.16.1.5

Type escape sequence to abort.
Sending 5, 100-byte ICMP Echos to 172.16.1.5, timeout is 2 seconds:
!!!!!
Success rate is 100 percent (5/5), round-trip min/avg/max = 20/33/60 ms
R3#ping 172.16.1.10

Type escape sequence to abort.
Sending 5, 100-byte ICMP Echos to 172.16.1.10, timeout is 2 seconds:
!!!!!
Success rate is 100 percent (5/5), round-trip min/avg/max = 20/28/40 ms
```

```
R4#ping 172.16.1.9

Type escape sequence to abort.
Sending 5, 100-byte ICMP Echos to 172.16.1.9, timeout is 2 seconds:
!!!!!
Success rate is 100 percent (5/5), round-trip min/avg/max = 20/36/52 ms
```

So all the pings to the neighbors are working. On R1 you can try pinging itself and it will successful too. If you disable the **frame-relay map ip 172.16.1.1 403 broadcast** command (use **no frame-relay map ip 172.16.1.1 403 broadcast**), R1 cannot ping itself anymore:

```
R1#ping 172.16.1.1

Type escape sequence to abort.
Sending 5, 100-byte ICMP Echos to 172.16.1.1, timeout is 2 seconds:
.....
Success rate is 0 percent (0/5)
```

In this Frame Relay lab we only set path for adjacent routers. We can't ping between R1 to R3 for example. There are two solutions so that R1 can ping R3:

+ Use multipoint subinterfaces on R2 (disable Inverse ARP and set two static frame-relay mappings on both R1 and R3)

+ Enable a routing protocol (static routing, EIGRP, OSPF, RIP…)

The GNS3 initial and final configs can be downloaded here:

Initial Configs:

https://www.dropbox.com/s/tsga9irmv6ciqur/Frame_Relay_TSHOOT_demo_initial.zip?dl=0

Final Configs:

https://www.dropbox.com/s/61cfpm5at56ozuj/Frame_Relay_TSHOOT_demo_finalConfigs.zip?dl=0

Some good references:

http://www.ciscopress.com/articles/article.asp?p=170741&seqNum=6

http://www.cisco.com/en/US/tech/tk713/tk237/technologies_q_and_a_item0 9186a008009457a.shtml

http://www.cisco.com/en/US/tech/tk713/tk237/technologies_tech_note09186 a008014f8a7.shtml

Next recommended reading: EIGRP over Frame Relay and EIGRP Redistribute Lab

EIGRP over Frame Relay and EIGRP Redistribute Lab

In the previous Frame Relay Point-to-Point Subinterface lab we have set up Layer 2 connection via Frame Relay but only adjacent routers can ping each other. For example R1 can ping R2 and R2 and ping R3 but R1 cannot ping R3. This is because R2 connects with R1 and R3 via point-to-point interfaces and they use separate subnets. In this lab we will use EIGRP to advertise these routes so that "remote" routers can ping each other.

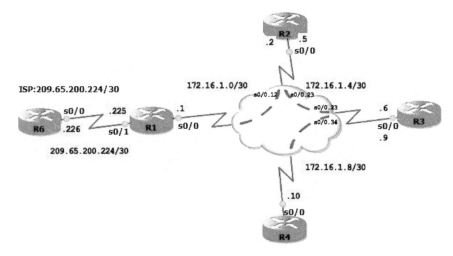

IOS used in this lab: **c3640-jk9s-mz.124-16.bin**

Tasks for this lab:

+ Configure EIGRP so that R1, R2, R3 and R4 can see and ping each other

+ Configure default route on R1 to 209.65.200.226 of R6

+ Advertise that default route to other routers via EIGRP so that every router can go to the Internet

Configure EIGRP on R1, R2, R3 and R4

R1	R2
router eigrp 16	router eigrp 16
network 172.16.0.0	network 172.16.1.0 0.0.0.255

R3	R4
router eigrp 16	router eigrp 16
network 172.16.1.4 0.0.0.3	network 172.16.1.0 0.0.0.25
network 172.16.1.9 0.0.0.0	

The configuration of EIGRP is simple but please keep in mind that the "network" command really doesn't advertise the network in that command. It enables EIGRP on the interface matched by the "network" command. For example, on R2 the "network 172.16.1.0 0.0.0.255" command instructs R2 to search all of its active interfaces (including subinterfaces) and R2 finds out the IP addresses of s0/0.12 and s0/0.23 subinterfaces belong to "172.16.10 0.0.0.255" network so R2 enables EIGRP on these subinterfaces. Another example is on R3, the "network 172.16.1.4 0.0.03" will enable EIGRP on s0/0.23 subinterface only. Without the "network 172.16.1.9 0.0.0.0" command, EIGRP would not be enabled on s0/0.34 subinterface. You can verify which interfaces are running EIGRP by the **show ip eigrp interfaces** command.

So any mask you put in your network command, as long as it matches or includes the IP address on a particular interface than you are good to go. And if you are lazy, just put the "network 0.0.0.0 255.255.255.255" command on each router, this will tell that router "enable EIGRP on all of my active interfaces (regardless what their IP addresses), please" because the wildcard 255.255.255.255 indicates that the router does not care about what network is using.

Note: The "network" command also works in the same way for OSPF, RIP and other Interior Gateway Protocol (IGP) routing protocols, except for BGP (which is an EGP routing protocol). In BGP, the function of a network statement is to tell the router to search the IP routing table for a particular network, and if that network is found, originate it into the BGP database.

After typing the configuration above we can ping remote routers now. For example the ping from R1 to R4 will be successful.

```
R1#ping 172.16.1.10

Type escape sequence to abort.
Sending 5, 100-byte ICMP Echos to 172.16.1.10, timeout is 2 seconds:
!!!!!
Success rate is 100 percent (5/5), round-trip min/avg/max = 60/72/108 ms
R1#
```

And the routing table of R1 contains all networks in this topology:

```
R1#show ip route
Codes: C - connected, S - static, R - RIP, M - mobile, B - BGP
       D - EIGRP, EX - EIGRP external, O - OSPF, IA - OSPF inter area
       N1 - OSPF NSSA external type 1, N2 - OSPF NSSA external type 2
       E1 - OSPF external type 1, E2 - OSPF external type 2
       i - IS-IS, su - IS-IS summary, L1 - IS-IS level-1, L2 - IS-IS level-2
       ia - IS-IS inter area, * - candidate default, U - per-user static route
       o - ODR, P - periodic downloaded static route

Gateway of last resort is not set

     172.16.0.0/30 is subnetted, 3 subnets
D       172.16.1.8 [90/3193856] via 172.16.1.2, 00:13:22, Serial0/0
D       172.16.1.4 [90/2681856] via 172.16.1.2, 00:13:22, Serial0/0
C       172.16.1.0 is directly connected, Serial0/0
R1#
```

Other routers' routing tables are the same so I will not post them here.

Redistribute static route into EIGRP

In this part we will learn how default route to Internet (or to ISP router)
should be advertised. Suppose R6 in the topology is the ISP router.

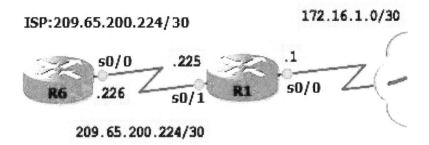

R1	R6
interface s0/1 ip address 209.65.200.225 255.255.255.252 no shutdown	interface s0/0 ip address 209.65.200.226 255.255.255.252 no shutdown ! interface Loopback0 ip address 209.65.200.241 255.255.255.252 ! //Static route to make sure R6 can reply to other routers ip route 172.16.0.0 255.255.0.0 209.65.200.225

You can't run an IGP routing protocol (like OSPF, EIGRP) on the ISP router so

the most simple way to send traffic to the ISP router is to use static route. So on R1 we will set up a static route to R6, we can do it via 3 ways:

R1(config)#ip route 0.0.0.0 0.0.0.0 s0/1

or

R1(config)#ip route 0.0.0.0 0.0.0.0 209.65.200.226

or

R1(config)#ip route 0.0.0.0 0.0.0.0 s0/1 209.65.200.226

Note: Just for your information about static route, the paragraph below is quoted from http://www.cisco.com/en/US/docs/security/asa/asa82/configuration/guide/route_static.html.

"Static routes remain in the routing table even if the specified gateway becomes unavailable. If the specified gateway becomes unavailable, you need to remove the static route from the routing table manually. However, static routes are removed from the routing table if the specified interface goes down, and are reinstated when the interface comes back up".

I want to notice that in all three cases of the ip route statements above, the static route will be removed in the routing table when s0/1 of R1 or s0/0 of R6 goes down. In other word, if you point a static route to a broadcast interface, the route is inserted into the routing table only when the broadcast interface is up.

As you see the third case use both the local outgoing interface and the next-hop IP address. In fact in the topology above it has no more effect than the second case (only use next-hop IP address). The third case is only better in the case the remote interface goes down and next-hop IP can be reachable through a recursive route (but I haven't test it).

For more information about "ip route" command, please read the following link: http://www.cisco.com/en/US/tech/tk365/technologies_tech_note09186a00800ef7b2.shtml

Ok, now R1 knows where to throw the packets when it can't find a suitable destination for them. The routing table of R1 now shows the default route to 209.65.200.226. Notice that by default, static routes have an Administrative Distance of 1.

```
R1#show ip route
Codes: C - connected, S - static, R - RIP, M - mobile, B - BGP
       D - EIGRP, EX - EIGRP external, O - OSPF, IA - OSPF inter area
       N1 - OSPF NSSA external type 1, N2 - OSPF NSSA external type 2
       E1 - OSPF external type 1, E2 - OSPF external type 2
       i - IS-IS, su - IS-IS summary, L1 - IS-IS level-1, L2 - IS-IS level-2
       ia - IS-IS inter area, * - candidate default, U - per-user static route
       o - ODR, P - periodic downloaded static route

Gateway of last resort is 209.65.200.226 to network 0.0.0.0

     172.16.0.0/30 is subnetted, 3 subnets
D       172.16.1.8 [90/3193856] via 172.16.1.2, 00:01:00, Serial0/0
D       172.16.1.4 [90/2681856] via 172.16.1.2, 00:01:00, Serial0/0
C       172.16.1.0 is directly connected, Serial0/0
     209.65.200.0/30 is subnetted, 1 subnets
C       209.65.200.224 is directly connected, Serial0/1
S*   0.0.0.0/0 [1/0] via 209.65.200.226
R1#
```

But R2, R3 and R4 still do not know! We can configure a static route on each of them but it is not a good thing to do. A better way to advertise this static route to R2, R3 and R4 is via the configured EIGRP. How can we do that? Ahh, we will redistribute this static route into EIGRP and EIGRP will advertise it for us. On R1:

router eigrp 16

redistribute static metric 64 100 100 100 1500

Note: The ip route command is not automatically carried in routing updates like the ip default-network command (in some routing protocols). You must redistribute the static command into a routing protocol for it to be carried.

The 5 parameters are used for redistribution into EIGRP are **Bandwidth, Delay, Reliability, Load, MTU**. For example the redistribution above is corresponding to **Bandwidth = 64Kbit, Delay = 1000ms, Reliability=100, Load=100, MTU=1500 bytes**. Notice that the unit of Delay used in the redistribution into EIGRP is tens of microsecond so we must divide Delay (in millisecond) by 10.

Now the routing tables of other routers (than R1) also learn this default route as an EIGRP external route (marked with **D*EX**). For example the routing table of R2:

```
R2#show ip route
Codes: C - connected, S - static, R - RIP, M - mobile, B - BGP
       D - EIGRP, EX - EIGRP external, O - OSPF, IA - OSPF inter area
       N1 - OSPF NSSA external type 1, N2 - OSPF NSSA external type 2
       E1 - OSPF external type 1, E2 - OSPF external type 2
       i - IS-IS, su - IS-IS summary, L1 - IS-IS level-1, L2 - IS-IS level-2
       ia - IS-IS inter area, * - candidate default, U - per-user static route
       o - ODR, P - periodic downloaded static route

Gateway of last resort is 172.16.1.1 to network 0.0.0.0

     172.16.0.0/30 is subnetted, 3 subnets
D        172.16.1.8 [90/2681856] via 172.16.1.6, 00:00:14, Serial0/0.23
C        172.16.1.4 is directly connected, Serial0/0.23
C        172.16.1.0 is directly connected, Serial0/0.12
D*EX 0.0.0.0/0 [170/40537600] via 172.16.1.1, 00:00:17, Serial0/0.12
```

The default administrative distance for EIGRP externals (routes redistributed into EIGRP) is 170.

By default, K1 = 1, K2 = 0, K3 = 1, K4 = 0, K5 = 0 so the metric formula for EIGRP is:

metric = (10^7 / Slowest Bandwidth of all interfaces[Kbit] + Sum of delay[ten-of-millisecond]) * 256

You can check the total delay and minimum bandwidth used to calculate EIGRP metric via the "show ip route <route>" command:

```
R2#show ip route 0.0.0.0
Routing entry for 0.0.0.0/0, supernet
  Known via "eigrp 16", distance 170, metric 40537600, candidate default path, type external
  Redistributing via eigrp 16
  Last update from 172.16.1.1 on Serial0/0.12, 00:00:23 ago
  Routing Descriptor Blocks:
  * 172.16.1.1, from 172.16.1.1, 00:00:23 ago, via Serial0/0.12
      Route metric is 40537600, traffic share count is 1
      Total delay is 21000 microseconds, minimum bandwidth is 64 Kbit
      Reliability 100/255, minimum MTU 1500 bytes
      Loading 100/255, Hops 1
```

Therefore the EIGRP metric here should be:

metric = (10^7 / 64 + 2100) * 256 = 40537600

Note: We are not sure why the unit of delay here is microsecond. But if we consider "microsecond" millisecond we will get the correct metric, otherwise we never get the correct result. And the unit of sum of delay used to calculate EIGRP metric is ten-of-millisecond so we have to divide the total delay by 10 (21000 / 10 = 2100).

We can verify R4 has learned the default route, too:

```
R4#show ip route
Codes: C - connected, S - static, R - RIP, M - mobile, B - BGP
       D - EIGRP, EX - EIGRP external, O - OSPF, IA - OSPF inter area
       N1 - OSPF NSSA external type 1, N2 - OSPF NSSA external type 2
       E1 - OSPF external type 1, E2 - OSPF external type 2
       i - IS-IS, su - IS-IS summary, L1 - IS-IS level-1, L2 - IS-IS level-2
       ia - IS-IS inter area, * - candidate default, U - per-user static route
       o - ODR, P - periodic downloaded static route

Gateway of last resort is 172.16.1.9 to network 0.0.0.0

     172.16.0.0/30 is subnetted, 3 subnets
C        172.16.1.8 is directly connected, Serial0/0
D        172.16.1.4 [90/2681856] via 172.16.1.9, 01:44:51, Serial0/0
D        172.16.1.0 [90/3193856] via 172.16.1.9, 01:44:51, Serial0/0
D*EX 0.0.0.0/0 [170/41561600] via 172.16.1.9, 00:00:20, Serial0/0
R4#
```

R4 also knows it has to route unknown traffic to 172.16.1.9. Also notice 172.16.1.9 now becomes the "gateway of last resort" of R4.

The GNS3 initial and final configs can be downloaded here:

Initial Configs:
https://www.dropbox.com/s/4bays4y0qgxhfsp/EIGRP_over_Frame_Relay_TSHOOT_Demo_initial.zip?dl=0

Final Configs:
https://www.dropbox.com/s/eb0jmi56uga42n4/EIGRP_over_Frame_Relay_TSHOOT_Demo_finalConfigs.zip?dl=0

Multiple Choice Questions

Question 1

Which command will limit debug output ppp authentication on serial 0/1 and serial 0/2?

A. debug condition interface range s0/1 -0/2

debug ppp authentication

B. debug condition interface s0/1 & 0/2

debug ppp authentication

C. debug int s0/1

debug int 0/2

debug ppp authentication

D. debug condition interface s0/1

debug condition interface s0/2

debug ppp authentication

Answer: D

Question 2

What is the MTU's size in a GRE tunnel?

A. 1450

B. 1460

C. 1476

D. 1470

Answer: C (20 bytes IP + 4 bytes MINIMUM GRE header))

Question 3

How to check MTU of interface using ping?

A. ping 10.1.1.1 size 1501

B. ping 10.1.1.1 size 1500 df-bit

C. ping 10.1.1.1 no-size

D. ping 10.1.1.1 size 1500

E. ping 10.1.1.1

Answer: B

Explanation

This command send ICMP packets with DF bit set. If the ping fails then there is problem with the path MTU. Another way to test the MTU of the interface is using the "sweep" keyword in extended "ping" command.

Question 4

The tunnel between R1 and R3 is not coming up. Which two statements are true? (choose two)

(Topology with a GRE tunnel and the outputs provided are show ip int brief and tunnel source and destination)

A. Tunnel source int Eth0/0 is down

B. No route from R1 to R3 loopback0

C. Source and destination not in same subnet

Answer: A B

Question 5

R1 and R2 OSPF neighbor. The outputs of the "show ip ospf neighbors" of these two routers are shown below. Which two statements are true? (choose two)

```
R1#show ip ospf neighbors
Neighbor ID    Pri  State         Dead Time  Address      Interface
192.168.1.2     1   FULL/DR       00:00:39   192.168.1.2  Ethernet0/0


R2#show ip ospf neighbors
Neighbor ID    Pri  State         Dead Time  Address      Interface
```

192.168.1.1   0 FULL/-   00:00:39 192.168.1.1   Ethernet0/0

A. They are not neighbors

B. R1 will not update its routes to R2

C. Interface Ethernet0/0 on router R2 is configured with ospf point-to-point command

D. They need to be configured as OSPF NBMA

E. R2 should be configured as stub

Answer: B C

Explanation

R2 shows "FULL/-" which means that its neighbor is configured in non-broadcast network. This is usually the result of the "ip ospf point-to-..." command on interface E0/0 of R2.

R1 shows "FULL/DR" which means it is configured in broadcast network. So the network types of R1 and R2 are mismatched which makes the advertising router unreachable and no routes update can be sent to other router.

There is another better explanation in the comment section so we also post it here for your reference. Special thanks to **Tamelir** for this explanation:

"You have to understand the output of "show ip ospf neighbor" command.

Most important part of it "State" doesn't shows the state of neighbor, as you would think. It shows the state of adjacency on side of the router where command is given.

So, when R2 shows that state of neighborhood with R1 "FULL/- " this means 2 things:

1.) Adjacency is in state FULL, databases are synced, we are neighbors. Both routers have passed through all states from INIT to FULL.

2.) The "/-" marks the network type of interface of router ON WHICH THE COMMAND IS GIVEN, not its neighbor.

So, state "FULL/-" on R2 means that R1 and R2 are neighbors, and the network type of interface Ethernet0/0 on **R2** is point-to-point, point-to-multipoint or point-to-multipoint nonbroadcast

State "FULL/DR " on R1 means that the network type of its E0/0 is either broadcast (default) or NBMA. It **thinks** that R2 is DR, only because broadcast network is multi-access and R1 selected itself as BDR. But R2 doesn't care, there was no DR/BDR selection on its side."

Question 6

Two routers are connected through PPP connection. After the PPP was established the admin put OSPF running above it. The OSPF formed adjacency but after soon the adjacency dropped. What is the reason?

A. MTU does not match

B. Area 0 need to exist for OSPF to function properly

C. GRE tunnel destination MUST not BE reachable through the tunnel

D. GRE tunnel ip address must be covered by network under "router ospf 1"

E. OSPF routes contains the route to tunnel destination

Answer: C

Question 7

Refer to the exhibit.

LO: 2.2.2.2/32   LO: 5.5.5.5/32

         192.168.1.0/24   192.168.2.0/24

R2   e0/0   e0/0 R4 e0/1   e0/0 R5

                            OSPF Area 0

R2#show ip route ospf	R5#show ip route ospf
O 192.168.2.0/24 [110/20] via 192.168.1.2	2.0.0.0/32 is subnetted, 1 subnets
	O 2.2.2.2 [110/21] via 192.168.2.1
R2#show run interface Tunnel0	
	O 192.168.1.0/24 [110/20] via 192.168.2.1
interface Tunnel0	
	R5#show run interface Tunnel0
ip address 10.0.0.1 255.255.255.252	
	interface Tunnel0
tunnel source Loopback0	
	ip address 10.0.0.2 255.255.255.252
tunnel destination 5.5.5.5	
	tunnel source Loopback0
end	
	tunnel destination 2.2.2.2
	end

The tunnel between R2 and R5 is not coming up. R2, R4, and R5 do not have any routing information sources other than OSPF and no route filtering is implemented anywhere in the network. Which two actions fix the issue? (Choose two)

A. Redistribute connected routes to OSPF on R5

B. Change the tunnel destination on R2 to 192.168.2.1

C. Advertise interface Lo0 to OSPF on R5

D. Configure a static route on R5 to 2.2 2.2 via 192.168.2.1

E. Fix the OSPF adjacency issue between R4 and R5

Answer: A C

BGP SIMLET

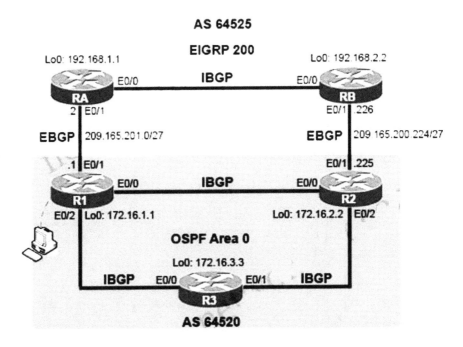

Question

Loopback0 is used for IBGP peering while physical interface address is used for EBGP. Identify the IBGP issues on R1 to R2, R3 and EBGP issues to RA and fix them so that the **show ip bgp** command on R1 will display all loopback interfaces of other routers.

Currently this simulator only supports show and ping commands. To fix the problem please type your commands into the textboxes below.

R1 running-config:

Currently this simulator only supports show and ping commands. To fix the problem
please type your commands into the textboxes below.
R1#show run
Building configuration...

Current configuration : 1442 bytes
!
! Last configuration change at 11:11:01 CET Wed Feb 8 2017
!
version 15.4
service timestamps debug datetime msec
service timestamps log datetime msec
no service password-encryption
!
hostname R1
!
boot-start-marker
boot-end-marker
!
aqm-register-fnf
!
!
no aaa new-model

clock timezone CET 1 0
mmi polling-interval 60
no mmi auto-configure
no mmi pvc
mmi snmp-timeout 180
!
!
!
!
!
!

!
!
!
ip cef
no ipv6 cef
!
multilink bundle-name authenticated
!
!
!
!

```
redundancy
!
!
!
!
!
!
!
!
!
!
!
!
!
interface Loopback0
 ip address 172.16.1.1 255.255.255.255
!
interface Ethernet0/0
 ip address 192.168.12.1 255.255.255.252
!
interface Ethernet0/1
 ip address 209.165.201.1 255.255.255.224
!

interface Ethernet0/2
 ip address 192.168.13.1 255.255.255.252
!
interface Ethernet0/3
 no ip address
 shutdown
!
router ospf 1
 network 172.16.1.1 0.0.0.0 area 0
 network 192.168.12.0 0.0.0.3 area 0
 network 192.168.13.0 0.0.0.3 area 0
!
router bgp 64520
 bgp log-neighbor-changes
 network 172.16.1.1 mask 255.255.255.255
 neighbor IBGP peer-group
 neighbor IBGP remote-as 64550
 neighbor IBGP update-source Loopback0
 neighbor 172.16.2.2 peer-group IBGP
 neighbor 172.16.3.3 peer-group IBGP
 neighbor 209.165.200.2 remote-as 64525
!
ip forward-protocol nd
!
!
```

```
no ip http server
no ip http secure-server
!
!
!
!
control-plane
!
!
!
!
!
!
!
line con 0
 logging synchronous
line aux 0
line vty 0 4
 login
 transport input none
!
!
end
R1#
```

Note: The configuration in the exam may be slightly different from this simulator so please grasp the concept well before taking the exam.

Solution

We see there are two issues here (two commands in bold), the first one is IBGP issue and the second one is EBGP issue.

R1(config)#router bgp 64520

R1(config-router)#neighbor IBGP remote-as 64520

R1(config-router)#no neighbor 209.165.200.2 remote-as 64525

R1(config-router)#neighbor 209.165.201.2 remote-as 64525

Note:

+ In the second statement we fix the IBGP group to "remote-as 64520" without removing the wrongly configured IBGP group ("neighbor IBGP remote-as 64550") because if we remove this statement, other related statements of IBGP (three statements "neighbor IBGP update-source Loopback0", "neighbor 172.16.2.2 peer-group IBGP", "neighbor 172.16.3.3 peer-group IBGP") will be removed automatically because IBGP group no longer exists.

+ Also in statement 2 the "IBGP" group must be written in capital. You will receive an error if writing it in lowercase.

After solving the problem don't forget to verify with the "show ip bgp" command.

Ticket 1 – OSPF Authentication

TSHOOT.com has created the test bed network shown in the layer 2 and layer 3 topology exhibits. This network consists of four routers, two layer 3 switches and two layer 2 switches.

In the IPv4 layer 3 topology, R1, R2, R3 and R4 are running OSPF with an OSPF process number 1. DSW1, DSW2 and R4 are running EIGRP with an AS of 10. Redistribution is enabled where necessary. R1 is running a BGP AS with a number of 65001. This AS has an eBGP connection to AS 65002 in the ISP's network. Because TSHOOT.com's address space is in the private range, R1 is also providing NAT translations between the inside(10.1.0.0/16 & 10.2.0.0/16)networks and the outside 209.65.200.0/24) network.

ASW1 and ASW 2 are layer 2 switches.

NTP is enabled on all devices with 209.65 200.226 serving as the master clock source.

The client workstations receive their IP address and default gateway via R4's DHCP server. The default gateway address of 10.2.1.254 is the IP address of HSRP group 10 which is running on DSW1 and DSW2.

In the IPv6 layer 3 topology, R1, R2, and R3 are running OSPFv3 with an OSPF process number 6. DSW1, DSW2 and R4 are running RIPng process name RIP_ZONE. The two IPv6 routing domains, OSPF 6 and RIPng are connected via GRE tunnel running over the underlying IPv4 OSPF domain. Redistribution is enabled where necessary.

The implementations group has been using the test bed to do a 'proof-of-concept' that requires both Client 1 and Client 2 to access the WEB Server at 209.65.200.241. After several changes to the network addressing, routing scheme, DHCP services, NTP services, layer 2 connectivity, FHRP services, and device security, a trouble ticket has been opened indicating that Client 1 cannot ping the 209.65.200.241 address.

Use the supported commands to isolated the cause of this fault and answer the questions.

CAUTION: Although trouble tickets may have similar fault indications, each ticket has its own issue and solution.

Popular questions about this ticket:

+ In this ticket, some readers asked why interface s0/0/0 on R1 is not running OSPF because the "network 10.1.1.0 0.0.0.3 area 12" is missing. In fact this interface is running OSPF with the "ip ospf 1 area 12" command configured under interface mode.

+ Also this is the only ticket that does not have the command "area 12 authentication message-digest" under "router ospf 1" so we need to "enable OSPF authentication on the s0/0/0 interface using the "ip ospf authentication message-digest" command" instead.

+ Some readers asked why the "traceroute 209.65.200.241" command on DSW1 stopped at 10.1.1.9 (R3), not 10.1.1.5 (R2). We explained as follows:

As you know, the fault is OSPF authentication on the link between R1 & R2. This fault causes R2 cannot receive the default route (advertised via the "default-information originate always" command on R1). R3 does not receive this default route either. Therefore R3 does not know how to reach 209.65.200.241. So when R3 receives the traceroute from DSW1, it simply drops it without forwarding it to R2. So R3 is the last hop to reply to DSW1.

+ So why does R4, without the default route (advertised from R1 as stated above), can still forward the ICMP packets to R3? This is because OSPF area 34 is configured as an OSPF Totally NSSA area. So R4 will send everything it does not know to R3 (its ABR).

1.Client is unable to ping R1's serial interface from the client.

Problem was disable authentication on R1, check where authentication is not given under router ospf of R1. (use ipv4 Layer 3)

Configuration of R1:

interface Serial0/0/0

description Link to R2

ip address 10.1.1.1 255.255.255.252

ip nat inside

encapsulation frame-relay

ip ospf message-digest-key 1 md5 TSHOOT

ip ospf network point-to-point

!

router ospf 1

router-id 1.1.1.1

log-adjacency-changes

network 10.1.2.0 0.0.0.255 area 12

network 10.1.10.0 0.0.0.255 area 12

default-information originate always

!

Configuration of R2:

interface Serial0/0/0.12 point-to-point

ip address 10.1.1.2 255.255.255.252

ip ospf authentication message-digest

ip ospf message-digest-key 1 md5 TSHOOT

!

Answer: on R1 need command "ip ospf authentication message-digest"

Ans1) R1

Ans2) IPv4 OSPF Routing

Ans3) Enable OSPF authentication on the s0/0/0 interface using the "ip ospf authentication message-digest" command.

Note:

There are two ways of configuring OSPF authentication:

interface Serial0/0/0

 ip ospf message-digest-key 1 md5 TSH00T

!

router ospf 1

 area 12 authentication message-digest

OR

interface Serial0/0/0

 ip ospf authentication message-digest

 ip ospf message-digest-key 1 md5 TSH00T

So you have to check carefully in both interface mode and "router ospf 1". If none of them has authentication then it is a fault.

Ticket 2 – HSRP Track (removed)

TSHOOT.com has created the test bed network shown in the layer 2 and layer 3 topology exhibits. This network consists of four routers, two layer 3 switches and two layer 2 switches.

In the IPv4 layer 3 topology, R1, R2, R3 and R4 are running OSPF with an OSPF process number 1. DSW1, DSW2 and R4 are running EIGRP with an AS of 10. Redistribution is enabled where necessary. R1 is running a BGP AS with a number of 65001. This AS has an eBGP connection to AS 65002 in the ISP's network. Because TSHOOT.com's address space is in the private range, R1 is also providing NAT translations between the inside(10.1.0.0/16 & 10.2.0.0/16)networks and the outside 209.65.200.0/24) network.

ASW1 and ASW 2 are layer 2 switches.

NTP is enabled on all devices with 209.65 200.226 serving as the master clock source.

The client workstations receive their IP address and default gateway via R4's DHCP server. The default gateway address of 10.2.1.254 is the IP address of HSRP group 10 which is running on DSW1 and DSW2.

In the IPv6 layer 3 topology, R1, R2, and R3 are running OSPFv3 with an OSPF process number 6. DSW1, DSW2 and R4 are running RIPng process name RIP_ZONE. The two IPv6 routing domains, OSPF 6 and RIPng are connected via GRE tunnel running over the underlying IPv4 OSPF domain. Redistribution is enabled where necessary.

Recently the implementation group has been using the test bed to do a 'proof-of-concept' that requires both Client1 and Client2 to access the WEB Server at 209.65.200.241. After several changes to the network addressing, routing schemes, DHCP services, NTP services, layer 2 connectivity, FHRP services, and, device security, a trouble ticket has been opened indicating DSW1 will not become the active router for HSRP group 10.

CAUTION: Although trouble tickets may have similar fault indications, each ticket has its own issue and solution.

HSRP was configured on DSW1 & DSW2. DSW1 is configured to be active but it does not become active.

Configuration of DSW1:

track 1 ip route 10.2.21.128 255.255.255.224 metric threshold

threshold metric up 1 down 2

!

track 10 ip route 10.1.21.128 255.255.255.224 metric threshold

threshold metric up 63 down 64

!

interface Vlan10

ip address 10.2.1.1 255.255.255.0

standby 10 ip 10.2.1.254

standby 10 priority 200

standby 10 preempt

standby 10 track 1 decrement 60

Answer: (use IPv4 Layer 3 Topology)

On DSW1 interface vlan 10 mode, type these commands:

no standby 10 track 1 decrement 60

standby 10 track 10 decrement 60

(ip for track command not exact for real exam)

Note: 10.1.21.129 is the IP address of a loopback interface on R4. This IP belongs to subnet 10.1.21.128/27.

Ans1) DSW1

Ans2) HSRP

Ans3) delete the command with track 1 and enter the command with track 10 (standby 10 track 10 decrement 60).

Ticket 3 – BGP Neighbor (removed)

TSHOOT.com has created the test bed network shown in the layer 2 and layer 3 topology exhibits. This network consists of four routers, two layer 3 switches and two layer 2 switches.

In the IPv4 layer 3 topology, R1, R2, R3 and R4 are running OSPF with an OSPF process number 1. DSW1, DSW2 and R4 are running EIGRP with an AS of 10. Redistribution is enabled where necessary. R1 is running a BGP AS with a number of 65001. This AS has an eBGP connection to AS 65002 in the ISP's network. Because TSHOOT.com's address space is in the private range, R1 is also providing NAT translations between the inside(10.1.0.0/16 & 10.2.0.0/16)networks and the outside 209.65.200.0/24) network.

ASW1 and ASW 2 are layer 2 switches.

NTP is enabled on all devices with 209.65 200.226 serving as the master clock source.

The client workstations receive their IP address and default gateway via R4's DHCP server. The default gateway address of 10.2.1.254 is the IP address of HSRP group 10 which is running on DSW1 and DSW2.

In the IPv6 layer 3 topology, R1, R2, and R3 are running OSPFv3 with an OSPF process number 6. DSW1, DSW2 and R4 are running RIPng process name RIP_ZONE. The two IPv6 routing domains, OSPF 6 and RIPng are connected via GRE tunnel running over the underlying IPv4 OSPF domain. Redistribution is enabled where necessary.

he implementations group has been using the test bed to do a 'proof-of-concept' that requires both Client 1 and Client 2 to access the WEB Server at 209.65.200.241. After several changes to the network addressing, routing scheme, DHCP services, NTP services, layer 2 connectivity, FHRP services, and device security, **a trouble ticket has ben opened indicating that Client 1 cannot ping the 209.65.200.241 address.**

Use the supported commands to isolated the cause of this fault and answer the questions.

CAUTION: Although trouble tickets may have similar fault indications, each ticket has its own issue and solution.

Problem: Client 1 is able to ping 209.65.200.226 but can't ping the Web Server 209.65.200.241.

Configuration of R1:

router bgp 65001

no synchronization

bgp log-neighbor-changes

network 209.65.200.224 mask 255.255.255.252

neighbor 209.56.200.226 remote-as 65002

no auto-summary

check bgp neighborship. **** show ip bgp sum****

The neighbor's address in the neighbor command is wrong under router BGP. (use ipv4 Layer 3)

Answer: need change on router mode on R1 neighbor 209.65.200.226

Ans1) R1

Ans2) BGP

Ans3) delete the wrong neighbor statement and enter the correct neighbor address in the neighbor command (change "neighbor 209.**56**.200.226 remote-as 65002" to "neighbor 209.**65**.200.226 remote-as 65002")

Ticket 4 – NAT Inside

TSHOOT.com has created the test bed network shown in the layer 2 and layer 3 topology exhibits. This network consists of four routers, two layer 3 switches and two layer 2 switches.

In the IPv4 layer 3 topology, R1, R2, R3 and R4 are running OSPF with an OSPF process number 1. DSW1, DSW2 and R4 are running EIGRP with an AS of 10. Redistribution is enabled where necessary. R1 is running a BGP AS with a number of 65001. This AS has an eBGP connection to AS 65002 in the ISP's network. Because TSHOOT.com's address space is in the private range, R1 is also providing NAT translations between the inside(10.1.0.0/16 & 10.2.0.0/16)networks and the outside 209.65.200.0/24) network.

ASW1 and ASW 2 are layer 2 switches.

NTP is enabled on all devices with 209.65 200.226 serving as the master clock source.

The client workstations receive their IP address and default gateway via R4's DHCP server. The default gateway address of 10.2.1.254 is the IP address of HSRP group 10 which is running on DSW1 and DSW2.

In the IPv6 layer 3 topology, R1, R2, and R3 are running OSPFv3 with an OSPF process number 6. DSW1, DSW2 and R4 are running RIPng process name RIP_ZONE. The two IPv6 routing domains, OSPF 6 and RIPng are connected via GRE tunnel running over the underlying IPv4 OSPF domain. Redistribution is enabled where necessary.

The implementations group has been using the test bed to do a 'proof-of-concept' that requires both Client 1 and Client 2 to access the WEB Server at 209.65.200.241. After several changes to the network addressing, routing scheme, DHCP services, NTP services, layer 2 connectivity, FHRP services, and device security, a trouble ticket has been opened indicating that Client 1 cannot ping the 209.65.200.241 address.

Use the supported commands to isolated the cause of this fault and answer the questions.

CAUTION: Although trouble tickets may have similar fault indications, each ticket has its own issue and solution.

Client 1 & 2 are not able to ping the web server 209.65.200.241, but all the routers & DSW1,2 can ping the server.

NAT problem on R1's ACL. (use IPv4 Layer 3)

Configuration of R1

ip nat inside source list nat_pool interface s0/0/1 overload

ip access-list standard nat_pool

 permit 10.1.0.0

 permit 10.2.0.0

 !

interface Serial0/0/1

ip address 209.65.200.225 255.255.255.252

ip nat outside

 !

interface Serial0/0/0.12

ip address 10.1.1.1 255.255.255.252

ip nat outside

ip ospf message-digest-key 1 md5 TSHOOT

ip ospf authentication message-digest

Ans1) R1

Ans2) NAT

Ans3) Under interface Serial0/0/0.12 delete the "ip nat outside" command and add the "ip nat inside" command.

Ticket 5 – R1 ACL

TSHOOT.com has created the test bed network shown in the layer 2 and layer 3 topology exhibits. This network consists of four routers, two layer 3 switches and two layer 2 switches.

In the IPv4 layer 3 topology, R1, R2, R3 and R4 are running OSPF with an OSPF process number 1. DSW1, DSW2 and R4 are running EIGRP with an AS of 10. Redistribution is enabled where necessary. R1 is running a BGP AS with a number of 65001. This AS has an eBGP connection to AS 65002 in the ISP's network. Because TSHOOT.com's address space is in the private range, R1 is also providing NAT translations between the inside(10.1.0.0/16 & 10.2.0.0/16)networks and the outside 209.65.200.0/24) network.

ASW1 and ASW 2 are layer 2 switches.

NTP is enabled on all devices with 209.65 200.226 serving as the master clock source.

The client workstations receive their IP address and default gateway via R4's DHCP server. The default gateway address of 10.2.1.254 is the IP address of HSRP group 10 which is running on DSW1 and DSW2.

n the IPv6 layer 3 topology, R1, R2, and R3 are running OSPFv3 with an OSPF process number 6. DSW1, DSW2 and R4 are running RIPng process name RIP_ZONE. The two IPv6 routing domains, OSPF 6 and RIPng are connected via GRE tunnel running over the underlying IPv4 OSPF domain. Redistribution is enabled where necessary.

The implementations group has been using the test bed to do a 'proof-of-concept' that requires both Client 1 and Client 2 to access the WEB Server at 209.65.200.241. After several changes to the network addressing, routing scheme, DHCP services, NTP services, layer 2 connectivity, FHRP services, and device security, a trouble ticket has been opened indicating that Client 1 cannot ping the 209.65.200.241 address.

Use the supported commands to isolated the cause of this fault and answer the questions.

CAUTION: Although trouble tickets may have similar fault indications, each ticket has its own issue and solution.

Configuration on R1

interface Serial0/0/1

description Link to ISP

ip address 209.65.200.225 255.255.255.252

ip nat outside

ip access-group edge_security in

!

ip access-list extended edge_security

deny ip 10.0.0.0 0.255.255.255 any

deny ip 172.16.0.0 0.15.255.255 any

deny ip 192.168.0.0 0.0.255.255 any

deny 127.0.0.0 0.255.255.255 any

permit ip host 209.65.200.241 any

!

Answer: add **permit ip 209.65.200.224 0.0.0.3 any** command to R1's ACL

Ans1) R1

Ans2) IPv4 Layer 3 Security

Ans3) Under the **ip access-list extended edge-security** configuration add the **permit ip 209.65.200.224 0.0.0.3 any** command

Note:

+ This is the only ticket the extended access-list edge_security exists. In other tickets, the access-list 30 is applied to the inbound direction of S0/0/1 of R1.

+ Although host 209.65.200.241 is permitted to go through the access-list (permit ip host 209.65.200.241 any) but clients cannot ping the web server because R1 cannot establish BGP session with neighbor 209.65.200.226.

Ticket 6 – VLAN filter

MarchTSHOOT.com has created the test bed network shown in the layer 2 and layer 3 topology exhibits. This network consists of four routers, two layer 3 switches and two layer 2 switches.

In the IPv4 layer 3 topology, R1, R2, R3 and R4 are running OSPF with an OSPF process number 1. DSW1, DSW2 and R4 are running EIGRP with an AS of 10. Redistribution is enabled where necessary. R1 is running a BGP AS with a number of 65001. This AS has an eBGP connection to AS 65002 in the ISP's network. Because TSHOOT.com's address space is in the private range, R1 is also providing NAT translations between the inside(10.1.0.0/16 & 10.2.0.0/16)networks and the outside 209.65.200.0/24) network.

ASW1 and ASW 2 are layer 2 switches.

NTP is enabled on all devices with 209.65 200.226 serving as the master clock source.

The client workstations receive their IP address and default gateway via R4's DHCP server. The default gateway address of 10.2.1.254 is the IP address of HSRP group 10 which is running on DSW1 and DSW2.

In the IPv6 layer 3 topology, R1, R2, and R3 are running OSPFv3 with an OSPF process number 6. DSW1, DSW2 and R4 are running RIPng process name RIP_ZONE. The two IPv6 routing domains, OSPF 6 and RIPng are connected via GRE tunnel running over the underlying IPv4 OSPF domain. Redistribution is enabled where necessary.

The implementations group has been using the test bed to do a 'proof-of-concept' that requires both Client 1 and Client 2 to access the WEB Server at 209.65.200.241. After several changes to the network addressing, routing scheme, DHCP services, NTP services, layer 2 connectivity, FHRP services, and device security, a trouble ticket has been opened indicating that Client 1 cannot ping the 209.65.200.241 address.

Use the supported commands to isolated the cause of this fault and answer the questions.

CAUTION: Although trouble tickets may have similar fault indications, each ticket has its own issue and solution.

Client 1 is not able to ping the server. Unable to ping DSW1 or the FTP Server(Use L2 Diagram).

Vlan Access map is applied on DSW1 blocking the ip address of client 10.2.1.3

Configuration on DSW1

vlan access-map test1 10

action drop

match ip address 10

```
 vlan access-map test1 20

action drop

match ip address 20

vlan access-map test1 30

action forward

match ip address 30

vlan access-map test1 40

action forward

!

vlan filter test1 vlan-list 10

!

access-list 10 permit 10.2.1.3

access-list 20 permit 10.2.1.4

access-list 30 permit 10.2.1.0 0.0.0.255

!

interface VLAN10

ip address 10.2.1.1 255.255.255.0
```

Ans1) DSW1

Ans2) VLAN ACL/Port ACL

Ans3) Under the global configuration mode enter no vlan filter test1 vlan-list 10 command.

Note: After choosing DSW1 for Ans1, next page (for Ans2) you have to scroll down to find the VLAN ACL/Port ACL option. The scroll bar only appears in this ticket and is very difficult to be seen.

Ticket 7 – Port Security (removed)

TSHOOT.com has created the test bed network shown in the layer 2 and layer 3 topology exhibits. This network consists of four routers, two layer 3 switches and two layer 2 switches.

In the IPv4 layer 3 topology, R1, R2, R3 and R4 are running OSPF with an OSPF process number 1. DSW1, DSW2 and R4 are running EIGRP with an AS of 10. Redistribution is enabled where necessary. R1 is running a BGP AS with a number of 65001. This AS has an eBGP connection to AS 65002 in the ISP's network. Because TSHOOT.com's address space is in the private range, R1 is also providing NAT translations between the inside(10.1.0.0/16 & 10.2.0.0/16)networks and the outside 209.65.200.0/24) network.

ASW1 and ASW 2 are layer 2 switches.

NTP is enabled on all devices with 209.65 200.226 serving as the master clock source.

The client workstations receive their IP address and default gateway via R4's DHCP server. The default gateway address of 10.2.1.254 is the IP address of HSRP group 10 which is running on DSW1 and DSW2.

In the IPv6 layer 3 topology, R1, R2, and R3 are running OSPFv3 with an OSPF process number 6. DSW1, DSW2 and R4 are running RIPng process name RIP_ZONE. The two IPv6 routing domains, OSPF 6 and RIPng are connected via GRE tunnel running over the underlying IPv4 OSPF domain. Redistribution is enabled where necessary.

The implementations group has been using the test bed to do a 'proof-of-concept' that requires both Client 1 and Client 2 to access the WEB Server at 209.65.200.241. After several changes to the network addressing, routing scheme, DHCP services, NTP services, layer 2 connectivity, FHRP services, and device security, <u>a trouble ticket has been opened indicating that Client 1 cannot ping the 209.65.200.241 address.</u>

Use the supported commands to isolated the cause of this fault and answer the questions.

CAUTION: Although trouble tickets may have similar fault indications, each ticket has its own issue and solution.

Client 1 is unable to ping Client 2 as well as DSW1. The command 'sh interfaces fa1/0/1' will show following message in the first line

'FastEthernet1/0/1 is down, line protocol is down (err-disabled)'

On ASW1 port-security mac 0000.0000.0001, interface in err-disable state

Configuration of ASW1

interface fa1/0/1

switchport access vlan 10

switchport mode access

switchport port-security

switchport port-security mac-address 0000.0000.0001

Answer: on ASW1 delete port-security & do on interfaces shutdown, no shutdown

Ans1) ASW1

Ans2) Port security

Ans3) In Configuration mode, using the interface range Fa1/0/1 – 2, then no switchport port-security, followed by shutdown, no shutdown interface configuration commands.

Ticket 8 – Switchport VLAN 10

TSHOOT.com has created the test bed network shown in the layer 2 and layer 3 topology exhibits. This network consists of four routers, two layer 3 switches and two layer 2 switches.

In the IPv4 layer 3 topology, R1, R2, R3 and R4 are running OSPF with an OSPF process number 1. DSW1, DSW2 and R4 are running EIGRP with an AS of 10. Redistribution is enabled where necessary. R1 is running a BGP AS with a number of 65001. This AS has an eBGP connection to AS 65002 in the ISP's network. Because TSHOOT.com's address space is in the private range, R1 is also providing NAT translations between the inside(10.1.0.0/16 & 10.2.0.0/16)networks and the outside 209.65.200.0/24) network.

ASW1 and ASW 2 are layer 2 switches.

NTP is enabled on all devices with 209.65 200.226 serving as the master clock source.

The client workstations receive their IP address and default gateway via R4's DHCP server. The default gateway address of 10.2.1.254 is the IP address of HSRP group 10 which is running on DSW1 and DSW2.

In the IPv6 layer 3 topology, R1, R2, and R3 are running OSPFv3 with an OSPF process number 6. DSW1, DSW2 and R4 are running RIPng process name RIP_ZONE. The two IPv6 routing domains, OSPF 6 and RIPng are connected via GRE tunnel running over the underlying IPv4 OSPF domain. Redistribution is enabled where necessary.

The implementations group has been using the test bed to do a 'proof-of-concept' that requires both Client 1 and Client 2 to access the WEB Server at 209.65.200.241. After several changes to the network addressing, routing scheme, DHCP services, NTP services, layer 2 connectivity, FHRP services, and device security, <u>a trouble ticket has been opened indicating that Client 1 cannot ping the 209.65.200.241 address.</u>

Use the supported commands to isolated the cause of this fault and answer the questions.

CAUTION: Although trouble tickets may have similar fault indications, each ticket has its own issue and solution.

Client 1 & 2 can't ping DSW1 or FTP Server but they are able to ping each other.

Configuration of ASW1

interface FastEthernet1/0/1

switchport mode access

!

interface FastEthernet1/0/2

switchport mode access

!

Interfaces Fa1/0/1 & Fa1/0/2 are in Vlan 1 (by default) but they should be in Vlan 10.

Answer:

Ans1)ASW1

Ans2)Vlan

Ans3)give command: interface range fa1/0/1-/2 & switchport access vlan 10

Ticket 9 – Switchport trunk

TSHOOT.com has created the test bed network shown in the layer 2 and layer 3 topology exhibits. This network consists of four routers, two layer 3 switches and two layer 2 switches.

In the IPv4 layer 3 topology, R1, R2, R3 and R4 are running OSPF with an OSPF process number 1. DSW1, DSW2 and R4 are running EIGRP with an AS of 10. Redistribution is enabled where necessary. R1 is running a BGP AS with a number of 65001. This AS has an eBGP connection to AS 65002 in the ISP's network. Because TSHOOT.com's address space is in the private range, R1 is also providing NAT translations between the inside(10.1.0.0/16 & 10.2.0.0/16)networks and the outside 209.65.200.0/24) network.

ASW1 and ASW 2 are layer 2 switches.

NTP is enabled on all devices with 209.65 200.226 serving as the master clock source.

The client workstations receive their IP address and default gateway via R4's DHCP server. The default gateway address of 10.2.1.254 is the IP address of HSRP group 10 which is running on DSW1 and DSW2.

In the IPv6 layer 3 topology, R1, R2, and R3 are running OSPFv3 with an OSPF process number 6. DSW1, DSW2 and R4 are running RIPng process name RIP_ZONE. The two IPv6 routing domains, OSPF 6 and RIPng are connected via GRE tunnel running over the underlying IPv4 OSPF domain. Redistribution is enabled where necessary.

The implementations group has been using the test bed to do a 'proof-of-concept' that requires both Client 1 and Client 2 to access the WEB Server at 209.65.200.241. After several changes to the network addressing, routing scheme, DHCP services, NTP services, layer 2 connectivity, FHRP services, and device security, a trouble ticket has been opened indicating that Client 1 cannot ping the 209.65.200.241 address.

Use the supported commands to isolated the cause of this fault and answer the questions.

CAUTION: Although trouble tickets may have similar fault indications, each ticket has its own issue and solution.

Client 1 & 2 can ping each other but they are unable to ping DSW1 or FTP Server (Use L2/3 Diagram)

Configuration of ASW1

interface PortChannel13

switchport mode trunk

switchport trunk allowed vlan 1-9 //Note: In fact you will see vlan 20,200 here but the concept is still the same

!

interface PortChannel23

switchport mode trunk

switchport trunk allowed vlan 1-9 //Note: In fact you will see vlan 20,200 here but the concept is still the same

!

interface FastEthernet1/0/1

switchport mode access

switchport access vlan 10

!

interface FastEthernet1/0/2

switchport mode access

switchport access vlan 10

Answer: on port channel 13, 23 disables all vlans and give **switchport trunk allowed vlan 10,200**

Ans1)ASW1

Ans2)Switch to switch connectivity

Ans3)int range portchannel13,portchannel23

switchport trunk allowed vlan none

switchport trunk allowed vlan 10,200

Ticket 10 – EIGRP AS (removed)

TSHOOT.com has created the test bed network shown in the layer 2 and layer 3 topology exhibits. This network consists of four routers, two layer 3 switches and two layer 2 switches.

In the IPv4 layer 3 topology, R1, R2, R3 and R4 are running OSPF with an OSPF process number 1. DSW1, DSW2 and R4 are running EIGRP with an AS of 10. Redistribution is enabled where necessary. R1 is running a BGP AS with a number of 65001. This AS has an eBGP connection to AS 65002 in the ISP's network. Because TSHOOT.com's address space is in the private range, R1 is also providing NAT translations between the inside(10.1.0.0/16 & 10.2.0.0/16)networks and the outside 209.65.200.0/24) network.

ASW1 and ASW 2 are layer 2 switches.

NTP is enabled on all devices with 209.65 200.226 serving as the master clock source.

The client workstations receive their IP address and default gateway via R4's DHCP server. The default gateway address of 10.2.1.254 is the IP address of HSRP group 10 which is running on DSW1 and DSW2.

In the IPv6 layer 3 topology, R1, R2, and R3 are running OSPFv3 with an OSPF process number 6. DSW1, DSW2 and R4 are running RIPng process name RIP_ZONE. The two IPv6 routing domains, OSPF 6 and RIPng are connected via GRE tunnel running over the underlying IPv4 OSPF domain. Redistribution is enabled where necessary.

The implementations group has been using the test bed to do a 'proof-of-concept' that requires both Client 1 and Client 2 to access the WEB Server at 209.65.200.241. After several changes to the network addressing, routing scheme, DHCP services, NTP services, layer 2 connectivity, FHRP services, and device security, a trouble ticket has been opened indicating that Client 1 cannot ping the 209.65.200.241 address.

Use the supported commands to isolated the cause of this fault and answer the questions.

CAUTION: Although trouble tickets may have similar fault indications, each ticket has its own issue and solution.

Note: This ticket (about Wrong EIGRP AS Number) does not appear in the exam nowadays and they are having problems so it is crossed out and please ignore it. (In fact in these tickets Clients cannot receive IP Addresses from DHCP Server).

Client 1 is not able to ping the Webserver

DSW1 can ping fa0/1 of R4 but can't ping s0/0/0.34

Check ip eigrp neighbors from DSW1 you will not see R4 as neighbor.(use ipv4 Layer 3)

'Show ip route' on DSW1 you will not see any 10.x.x.x network route.

On DSW1 & DWS2 the EIGRP AS number is 10 (router eigrp 10) but on R4 it is 1 (router eigrp 1)

Answer: change router AS on R4 from 1 to 10

Ans1) R4

Ans2) EIGRP

Ans3) Change EIGRP AS number from 1 to 10

Ticket 11 – OSPF to EIGRP

TSHOOT.com has created the test bed network shown in the layer 2 and layer 3 topology exhibits. This network consists of four routers, two layer 3 switches and two layer 2 switches.

In the IPv4 layer 3 topology, R1, R2, R3 and R4 are running OSPF with an OSPF process number 1. DSW1, DSW2 and R4 are running EIGRP with an AS of 10. Redistribution is enabled where necessary. R1 is running a BGP AS with a number of 65001. This AS has an eBGP connection to AS 65002 in the ISP's network. Because TSHOOT.com's address space is in the private range, R1 is also providing NAT translations between the inside(10.1.0.0/16 & 10.2.0.0/16)networks and the outside 209.65.200.0/24) network.

ASW1 and ASW 2 are layer 2 switches.

NTP is enabled on all devices with 209.65 200.226 serving as the master clock source.

The client workstations receive their IP address and default gateway via R4's DHCP server. The default gateway address of 10.2.1.254 is the IP address of HSRP group 10 which is running on DSW1 and DSW2.

In the IPv6 layer 3 topology, R1, R2, and R3 are running OSPFv3 with an OSPF process number 6. DSW1, DSW2 and R4 are running RIPng process name RIP_ZONE. The two IPv6 routing domains, OSPF 6 and RIPng are connected via GRE tunnel running over the underlying IPv4 OSPF domain. Redistribution is enabled where necessary.

The implementations group has been using the test bed to do a 'proof-of-concept' that requires both Client 1 and Client 2 to access the WEB Server at 209.65.200.241. After several changes to the network addressing, routing scheme, DHCP services, NTP services, layer 2 connectivity, FHRP services, and device security, a trouble ticket has been opened indicating that Client 1 cannot ping the 209.65.200.241 address.

Use the supported commands to isolated the cause of this fault and answer the questions.

CAUTION: Although trouble tickets may have similar fault indications, each ticket has its own issue and solution.

Note: Currently the above link is not correct. We will update it soon.

On R4:

router eigrp 10

 redistribute ospf 1 **route-map OSPF->EIGRP**

network 10.1.4.0 0.0.0.255

network 10.1.10.0 0.0.0.255

network 10.1.21.128 0.0.0.3

default-metric 100000 100 100 1 1500

no auto-summary

!

router ospf 1

network 10.1.1.8 0.0.0.0 area 34

redistribute eigrp 10 subnets

!

route-map OSPF_to_EIGRP

match ip address 1

Ans1) R4

Ans2) IPv4 Route Redistribution

Ans3) Under the EIGRP process, delete the **redistribute ospf 1 route-map OSPF->EIGRP** command and enter the **redistribute ospf 1 route-map OSPF_to_EIGRP** command.

Explanation for this ticket:

In this topology, we are doing mutual redistribution at multiple points (between OSPF and EIGRP on R4, DSW1 & DSW2), which is a very common cause of network problems, especially routing loops so you should use route-map to prevent redistributed routes from redistributing again into the original domain.

In this ticket, route-map is also used for this purpose. For example, the route-map "EIGRP_to_OSPF" is used to prevent any routes that have been redistributed into OSPF from redistributed again into EIGRP domain by tagging these routes with tag 90. These routes are prevented from redistributing again by route-map OSPF_to_EIGRP by denying any routes with tag 90 set.

Therefore in this ticket, typing a wrong route-map (which does not exist) may cause problem.

Ticket 12 – IPv6 OSPF

TSHOOT.com has created the test bed network shown in the layer 2 and layer 3 topology exhibits. This network consists of four routers, two layer 3 switches and two layer 2 switches.

In the IPv4 layer 3 topology, R1, R2, R3 and R4 are running OSPF with an OSPF process number 1. DSW1, DSW2 and R4 are running EIGRP with an AS of 10. Redistribution is enabled where necessary. R1 is running a BGP AS with a number of 65001. This AS has an eBGP connection to AS 65002 in the ISP's network. Because TSHOOT.com's address space is in the private range, R1 is also providing NAT translations between the inside(10.1.0.0/16 & 10.2.0.0/16)networks and the outside 209.65.200.0/24) network.

ASW1 and ASW 2 are layer 2 switches.

NTP is enabled on all devices with 209.65 200.226 serving as the master clock source.

The client workstations receive their IP address and default gateway via R4's DHCP server. The default gateway address of 10.2.1.254 is the IP address of HSRP group 10 which is running on DSW1 and DSW2.

In the IPv6 layer 3 topology, R1, R2, and R3 are running OSPFv3 with an OSPF process number 6. DSW1, DSW2 and R4 are running RIPng process name RIP_ZONE. The two IPv6 routing domains, OSPF 6 and RIPng are connected via GRE tunnel running over the underlying IPv4 OSPF domain. Redistribution is enabled where necessary.

Recently the implementation group has been using the test bed to do an IPv6 'proof-of-concept'. After several changes to the network addressing and routing schemes, <u>a trouble ticket has been opened indicating that the loopback address on R1 (2026::111:1) is not able to ping the loopback address on DSW2 (2026::102:1).</u>

Use the supported commands to isolated the cause of this fault and answer the questions.

CAUTION: Although trouble tickets may have similar fault indications, each ticket has its own issue and solution.

DSW1 & R4 can't ping R2's loopback interface or s0/0/0.12 IPv6 address.

R2 is not an OSPFv3 neighbor on R3

Situation: ipv6 ospf was not enabled on R2's serial interface connecting to R3. (use ipv6 Layer 3)

Configuration of R2

ipv6 router ospf 6

router-id 2.2.2.2

!

interface s0/0/0.23

ipv6 address 2026::1:1/122

Configuration of R3

ipv6 router ospf 6

router-id 3.3.3.3

!

interface s0/0/0.23

ipv6 address 2026::1:2/122

ipv6 ospf 6 area 0

Answer:

In interface configuration mode of s0/0/0.23 on R2:

ipv6 ospf 6 area 12

Ans1) R2

Ans2) IPv6 OSPF Routing

Ans3) Under the interface Serial 0/0/0.23 configuration enter the 'ipv6 ospf 6 area 0' command. (notice that it is "area 0", not "area 12")

Ticket 13 – DHCP Helper-address

TSHOOT.com has created the test bed network shown in the layer 2 and layer 3 topology exhibits. This network consists of four routers, two layer 3 switches and two layer 2 switches.

In the IPv4 layer 3 topology, R1, R2, R3 and R4 are running OSPF with an OSPF process number 1. DSW1, DSW2 and R4 are running EIGRP with an AS of 10. Redistribution is enabled where necessary. R1 is running a BGP AS with a number of 65001. This AS has an eBGP connection to AS 65002 in the ISP's network. Because TSHOOT.com's address space is in the private range, R1 is also providing NAT translations between the inside(10.1.0.0/16 & 10.2.0.0/16)networks and the outside 209.65.200.0/24) network.

ASW1 and ASW 2 are layer 2 switches.

NTP is enabled on all devices with 209.65 200.226 serving as the master clock source.

The client workstations receive their IP address and default gateway via R4's DHCP server. The default gateway address of 10.2.1.254 is the IP address of HSRP group 10 which is running on DSW1 and DSW2.

In the IPv6 layer 3 topology, R1, R2, and R3 are running OSPFv3 with an OSPF process number 6. DSW1, DSW2 and R4 are running RIPng process name RIP_ZONE. The two IPv6 routing domains, OSPF 6 and RIPng are connected via GRE tunnel running over the underlying IPv4 OSPF domain. Redistribution is enabled where necessary.

The implementations group has been using the test bed to do a 'proof-of-concept' that requires both Client 1 and Client 2 to access the WEB Server at 209.65.200.241. After several changes to the network addressing, routing scheme, DHCP services, NTP services, layer 2 connectivity, FHRP services, and device security, a trouble ticket has been opened indicating that Client 1 cannot ping the 209.65.200.241 address.

Use the supported commands to isolated the cause of this fault and answer the questions.

CAUTION: Although trouble tickets may have similar fault indications, each ticket has its own issue and solution.

Note: Currently the link above is not up-to-date. We will update it soon.

Configuration on DSW1:

!

interface Vlan 10

ip address 10.2.1.1 255.255.255.0

ip helper-address 10.2.21.129

!

Note: In this ticket you will find port-security configured on ASW1 but it is not the problem.

Ans1) DSW1

Ans2) IP DHCP Server (or DHCP)

Ans3) on DSW1 delete "ip helper-address 10.2.21.129" and apply "ip helper-address 10.1.21.129" command

Ticket 14 – EIGRP Passive Interface

TSHOOT.com has created the test bed network shown in the layer 2 and layer 3 topology exhibits. This network consists of four routers, two layer 3 switches and two layer 2 switches.

In the IPv4 layer 3 topology, R1, R2, R3 and R4 are running OSPF with an OSPF process number 1. DSW1, DSW2 and R4 are running EIGRP with an AS of 10. Redistribution is enabled where necessary. R1 is running a BGP AS with a number of 65001. This AS has an eBGP connection to AS 65002 in the ISP's network. Because TSHOOT.com's address space is in the private range, R1 is also providing NAT translations between the inside(10.1.0.0/16 & 10.2.0.0/16)networks and the outside 209.65.200.0/24) network.

ASW1 and ASW 2 are layer 2 switches.

NTP is enabled on all devices with 209.65 200.226 serving as the master clock source.

The client workstations receive their IP address and default gateway via R4's DHCP server. The default gateway address of 10.2.1.254 is the IP address of HSRP group 10 which is running on DSW1 and DSW2.

In the IPv6 layer 3 topology, R1, R2, and R3 are running OSPFv3 with an OSPF process number 6. DSW1, DSW2 and R4 are running RIPng process name RIP_ZONE. The two IPv6 routing domains, OSPF 6 and RIPng are connected via GRE tunnel running over the underlying IPv4 OSPF domain. Redistribution is enabled where necessary.

The implementations group has been using the test bed to do a 'proof-of-concept' that requires both Client 1 and Client 2 to access the WEB Server at 209.65.200.241. After several changes to the network addressing, routing scheme, DHCP services, NTP services, layer 2 connectivity, FHRP services, and device security, a trouble ticket has been opened indicating that Client 1 cannot ping the 209.65.200.241 address.

Use the supported commands to isolated the cause of this fault and answer the questions.

CAUTION: Although trouble tickets may have similar fault indications, each ticket has its own issue and solution.

Note: In this ticket you will notice that both Clients still get IP addresses (10.2.1.x) from DHCP Server but in real life they cannot get IP addresses (we have tested with real devices). It is a bug of the exam!

the neighborship between R4 and DSW1 wasn't establised. Client 1 can't ping R4

Configuration on R4:

router eigrp 10

 passive-interface default

 redistribute ospf 1 route-map OSPF->EIGRP

 network 10.1.4.4 0.0.0.3

 network 10.1.4.8 0.0.0.3

 network 10.1.21.128 0.0.0.3

 default-metric 10000 100 255 1 10000

 no auto-summary

Answer 1) R4

Answer 2) IPv4 EIGRP Routing

Answer 3) enter no passive interface for interfaces connected to DSW1 under EIGRP process (or in Interface f0/1 and f0/0, something like this)

Note: There is a loopback interface on this device which has an IP address of 10.1.21.129 so we have to include the "network 10.1.21.128 0.0.0.3" command.

* Just for your information, in fact Clients 1 & 2 in this ticket CANNOT receive IP addresses from DHCP Server because DSW1 cannot reach 10.1.21.129 (an loopback interface on R4) because of the "passive-interface default" command. But in the exam you will see that Clients 1 & 2 can still get their IP addresses! It is a bug in the exam.

Ticket 15 – IPv6 GRE Tunnel

TSHOOT.com has created the test bed network shown in the layer 2 and layer 3 topology exhibits. This network consists of four routers, two layer 3 switches and two layer 2 switches.

In the IPv4 layer 3 topology, R1, R2, R3 and R4 are running OSPF with an OSPF process number 1. DSW1, DSW2 and R4 are running EIGRP with an AS of 10. Redistribution is enabled where necessary. R1 is running a BGP AS with a number of 65001. This AS has an eBGP connection to AS 65002 in the ISP's network. Because TSHOOT.com's address space is in the private range, R1 is also providing NAT translations between the inside(10.1.0.0/16 & 10.2.0.0/16)networks and the outside 209.65.200.0/24) network.

ASW1 and ASW 2 are layer 2 switches.

NTP is enabled on all devices with 209.65 200.226 serving as the master clock source.

The client workstations receive their IP address and default gateway via R4's DHCP server. The default gateway address of 10.2.1.254 is the IP address of HSRP group 10 which is running on DSW1 and DSW2.

In the IPv6 layer 3 topology, R1, R2, and R3 are running OSPFv3 with an OSPF process number 6. DSW1, DSW2 and R4 are running RIPng process name RIP_ZONE. The two IPv6 routing domains, OSPF 6 and RIPng are connected via GRE tunnel running over the underlying IPv4 OSPF domain. Redistribution is enabled where necessary.

Recently the implementation group has been using the test bed to do an IPv6 'proof-of-concept'. After several changes to the network addressing and routing schemes, a trouble ticket has been opened indicating that the loopback address on R1 (2026::111:1) is not able to ping the loopback address on DSW2 (2026::102:1).

Use the supported commands to isolated the cause of this fault and answer the questions.

CAUTION: Although trouble tickets may have similar fault indications, each ticket has its own issue and solution.

Problem: Loopback address on R1 (2026::111:1) is not able to ping the loopback address on DSW2 (2026::102:1).

Configuration of R3:

!

interface Tunnel34

no ip address

ipv6 address 2026::34:1/122

ipv6 enable

ipv6 ospf 6 area 34

tunnel source Serial0/0/0.34

tunnel destination 10.1.1.10

tunnel mode ipv6

!

Configuration of R4:

interface Tunnel34

no ip address

ipv6 address 2026::34:2/122

ipv6 enable

ipv6 ospf 6 area 34

tunnel source Serial0/0/0

tunnel destination 10.1.1.9

!

Answer:

Ans1) R3

Ans2) Ipv4 and Ipv6 Interoperability

Ans3) Under the interface Tunnel34, remove 'tunnel mode ipv6' command

Ticket 16 - IPv6 RIPng OSPFv3 Redistribution

TSHOOT.com has created the test bed network shown in the layer 2 and layer 3 topology exhibits. This network consists of four routers, two layer 3 switches and two layer 2 switches.

In the IPv4 layer 3 topology, R1, R2, R3 and R4 are running OSPF with an OSPF process number 1. DSW1, DSW2 and R4 are running EIGRP with an AS of 10. Redistribution is enabled where necessary. R1 is running a BGP AS with a number of 65001. This AS has an eBGP connection to AS 65002 in the ISP's network. Because TSHOOT.com's address space is in the private range, R1 is also providing NAT translations between the inside(10.1.0.0/16 & 10.2.0.0/16)networks and the outside 209.65.200.0/24) network.

ASW1 and ASW 2 are layer 2 switches.

NTP is enabled on all devices with 209.65 200.226 serving as the master clock source.

The client workstations receive their IP address and default gateway via R4's DHCP server. The default gateway address of 10.2.1.254 is the IP address of HSRP group 10 which is running on DSW1 and DSW2.

In the IPv6 layer 3 topology, R1, R2, and R3 are running OSPFv3 with an OSPF process number 6. DSW1, DSW2 and R4 are running RIPng process name RIP_ZONE. The two IPv6 routing domains, OSPF 6 and RIPng are connected via GRE tunnel running over the underlying IPv4 OSPF domain. Redistribution is enabled where necessary.

Recently the implementation group has been using the test bed to do an IPv6 'proof-of-concept'. After several changes to the network addressing and routing schemes, a trouble ticket has been opened indicating that the loopback address on R1 (2026::111:1) is not able to ping the loopback address on DSW2 (2026::102:1).

Use the supported commands to isolated the cause of this fault and answer the questions.

CAUTION: Although trouble tickets may have similar fault indications, each ticket has its own issue and solution.

Problem: Loopback address on R1 (2026::111:1) is not able to ping the loopback address on DSW2 (2026::102:1).

Configuration of R4:

ipv6 router ospf 6

log-adjacency-changes

!

ipv6 router rip RIP_ZONE

redistribute ospf 6 metric 2 include-connected

!

Answer:

Ans1) R4

Ans2) Ipv6 OSPF Routing

Ans3) Under ipv6 ospf process add the 'redistribute rip RIP_Zone include-connected' command

Practice TSHOOT Tickets with Packet Tracer

Now you can practice most TSHOOT Tickets with Packet Tracer v6.1.
Please download all the tickets in one file here:
https://www.dropbox.com/s/8yt3a151hf062l1/Cisco_PT_6_1_TSHOOT_Package.zip?dl=0.

All the guides were included in that file.

Note: Please use at least the final Packet Tracer v6.1 (STUDENT Release) or above to open them. Below is a screenshot of the pkt files:

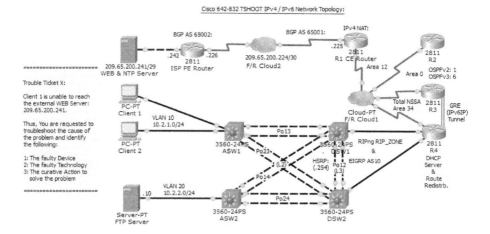

Cisco 642-832 TSHOOT IPv4 / IPv6 Network Topology:

GOOD LUCK!!